WHY CAMPUS MINISTRY

How one denomination organized a national
campus ministry that has become a major
Christian student movement

DENNIS GAYLOR
JOHN W. KENNEDY

Cover Design – Jaycee DeLorenzo
Publishing Coordinator – Sharon Kizziah-Holmes

Indie Pub Press
Springfield, MO

ISBN -13: 978-1-960499-13-4

TABLE OF CONTENTS

FOREWORD

I had never taken a single class or heard a single lecture at a secular college, or even been on such a college campus except for taking the S.A.T. at Franklin and Marshall College in Lancaster, Pennsylvania. But when Rick Howard, national leader of Chi Alpha, came to our youth convention in 1966 and said the Assemblies of God was now doing ministry on secular college campuses, my heart leaped within me!

On graduating a few months later from seminary, working as a full-time unpaid volunteer with Chi Alpha felt better than any salaried ministry post available. We toured Pennsylvania campuses, and met with students.

After over a year, we went to a church with a secular college ministry, with dynamic young people who still lead in ministry.

A couple years later, we came to lead Chi Alpha at national headquarters, and found a small group of people like ourselves, who, like those of 1 Samuel 10:26, were "a band of men whose hearts God had touched" to help with the coming of the Kingdom on the campus. That group grew. God touched more hearts.

One young couple in that "band of men and women" came from Texas. When we needed to expand, Dennis and Barbara Gaylor were the ones who came to do it. Their hearts had been touched by God for the task.

Dennis became the long-term national Chi Alpha director, with unique creativity and courage, a man who led the ministry into a growth and complexity that still astonishes me!

Dennis, and John Kennedy, are presenting here stories of others whose hearts, sometimes to their great surprise, have been touched by God to work toward the kingdom of God coming to the secular university campus.

Beware as you read it. Life-changing heart touching is still going on.

Dave Gable, March 2023

National Director, Chi Alpha Campus Ministries, 1971-1979

INTRODUCTION

Why campus ministry?

This book answers this question through a condensed decade by decade history of the Assemblies of God (AG) student ministry, Chi Alpha, 1953-2023, combined with 15 contemporary campus ministry stories.

Open to New Ideas

The campus is the most strategic mission field for communicating the good news to college students who are open like no other time to consider Christianity. During their life stage, they are making important lifetime decisions. They are searching for meaning and purpose and truth.

Tomorrow's Leaders

Universities create tomorrow's leaders in politics, medicine, business, technology, and every aspect of societal life. Every race, creed, culture, language, philosophy, and religion are represented on today's colleges and universities. The university has more influence on the direction, morality, and overall fabric of society than any other institution on the face of the earth.

Student Awakenings

Another reason the campus is strategic is it has been marked by campus revivals and student awakenings. When students seek the Lord and experience His salvation and learn about Christianity, they read His Word and pray, and obey the Scripture's teaching. These students are often the forerunners of renewal and revival on campus. When these students gather on campus in a residence hall lounge, campus café, classroom, and the student center to pray and allow the

Holy Spirit to speak to and guide them, it is not surprising that they become a catalyst for spiritual stirrings that can lead to God spiritually moving by the Holy Spirit.

International Students

International students coming to the U.S. for study and training is another reason why campus ministry is significant and strategic. The world is at our doorstep. More than 1 million international students from almost 200 nations are on campuses across the U.S. American students can make friendships with international students without needing a passport, visa, or knowledge of their language, culture, or customs. International students have come to the U.S. on their own expense or sponsored by their government to study in our institutions of higher education. The reverse works. When international students are befriended and influenced by Christians, with many coming to faith in Jesus Christ, they will return to their home country without needing a passport, visa, or to learn the language or culture.

Chi Alpha developed from a handful of students in the 1950s on one campus — to several hundred campuses with established Chi Alpha ministries by 2023. Chi Alpha is a major student movement.

Part I written by myself, Dennis Gaylor, captures the historical events of each decade that grew this nationwide ministry, and **Part II** written by John W. Kennedy, includes current narratives as campus ministers tell their stories.

PART I — CHI ALPHA

A HISTORY

Part I of the book tells the story of Chi Alpha's organizational development from 1947 to present 2023, a 76-year period divided into decades from the beginning, envisioned, to today, epic. It introduces the national leaders, programs, methodologies, and events that created a Chi Alpha culture and campus ministry movement. It began with a handful of students on one campus in 1953, and has grown to 289 chartered campus groups involving 16,028 students.

Envision 1940s

1,720 colleges and universities
1,494,000 college students
No data on international students studying
on U.S. campuses
No chartered Chi Alpha groups
U.S. population: 132,164,569

What happened in the 1940s?

Franklin D. Roosevelt (1933-1945) and Harry S. Truman (1945-1953) were presidents. Radio was the lifeline for Americans. Great Depression. Dec. 7, 1941, Japanese bombed Pearl Harbor and U.S. entered World War II. Rationing. Japanese immigrants sent to internment camps. Women needed to replace men who had gone off to war, so the first great exodus of women from home to the workplace began. Penicillin revolutionized medicine. Atom bomb. The G.I. Bill entitled returning soldiers to a college education. Start of the Baby Boom. The decade began with inexpensive paperback books. Teenagers became a recognized force in the '40s. The Supreme Court rules discrimination against Blacks voting is unconstitutional. Holocaust. Big Bands dominated popular music: Glenn Miller, Tommy Dorsey, Duke Ellington, and Benny Goodman. Jitterbug. The Slinky. Cold War begins. Individual singers struck out on their own: Bing Crosby, Frank Sinatra, Perry Como. At the end of WWII there were 5,000 TV sets with five-inch black and white screens.

CHAPTER 1

Envision 1940s

Modern-Day Pentecostal Movement

The Assemblies of God (AG) was birthed in the fires of revival that swept the world at the turn of the 20th century. Participants in the revival were filled with the Holy Spirit in similar fashion to the disciples and followers of Jesus on the Jewish Feast of Pentecost (Acts 2:38-39). Participants were called "Pentecostals."

Like those in the Upper Room, the followers of the 20th century revival spoke in tongues as they received the baptism of the Holy Spirit. Other supernatural manifestations such as prophecy, interpretations, spiritual conversion, and healings also took place.

As early as 1901, reports of the baptism in the Holy Spirit were observed. The winds of the Spirit carried the revival from the Midwest, to the South, and to the Western regions of North America, and eventually swept around the world.*

*The Assemblies of God was founded in 1914. Today there are 13,000 churches in the U.S with 3 million members and adherents. There are 69 million AG members worldwide, making the AG the world's largest Pentecostal denomination.

As early as 1913, a Pentecostal publication called for persons and churches experiencing this modern-day move of the Holy Spirit to meet together for the purpose of fellowship and doctrinal unity. Other reasons to gather included facilitating missionaries, chartering churches, and forming Bible training schools.

The Assemblies of God Organizes

The first meeting was held in Hot Springs, Arkansas, in April 1914. This meeting brought together 300 church leaders, and consisted of three days of prayer and preaching before any business. Apprehensive about creating another denomination, those attending agreed to form a loosely knit fellowship of independent churches. So began the General Council of the AG.

What does the move of the Holy Spirit and the Assemblies of God have to do with Chi Alpha Campus Ministries? Chi Alpha represents an expression on today's secular college and university campuses of the modern Pentecostal movement that marked the beginning of the 20th century. It was 33 years later (1947) after a tidal wave of G.I.s from WWII flooded the colleges and universities that an effort to develop a program to minister to AG college students was initiated.

Prior to 1940, the American universities were primarily the domain of elite young people from middle and upper class families, and mostly men. In 1944, Congress passed the G.I. Bill, which made it possible for WWII veterans to attend college for free. The campuses were inundated with students, and denominations and churches took notice. How was the Church going to reach these young people coming back from the war without the habits of home and family values and church values?

J. Robert Ashcroft, a young instructor at Central Bible Institute (CBI) in Springfield, Missouri, expressed concern for the spiritual life of AG youth attending non-AG institutions of higher education. Never before had so many AG young people headed off to college. Ashcroft was concerned that the values of young people coming back from WWII had started to change. They were being influenced by secular views, infidelity, and atheism.

The Formation of a College Ministries Division

Ashcroft brought his concerns to the fifth AG National Sunday School Convention in February 1947. He led a discussion on young people and challenged the AG to develop a program that would minister to AG youth attending colleges outside the Fellowship.

In 1948, the National Christ's Ambassadors (CAs) Department established a college ministries division and launched a duplicated paper, the *College Fellowship Bulletin (CFB)*. A handful of editors from other departments at AG headquarters snatched moments from other responsibilities to write articles and edit the *CFB* and shepherd the college division in its infancy. Many AG young people were completely cut off — perhaps for the first time — from Pentecostal fellowship when they entered a college or university. This newsletter provided a link for AG youth attending secular colleges to connect to the denomination and other AG students.

Each issue of *CFB* listed AG students and the campuses they represented. College students receiving the bulletin were encouraged that the Church stood with them in prayer and concerned for their spiritual welfare. By the end of the May 1949 academic year, the bulletin reported 239 AG students representing 95 colleges.

AG leaders realized that sending the *CFB* to collegians had limited influence. The need to organize AG students on campus, connect them with each other, and bring an effective Christian witness to campus was apparent.

It should be noted that early in the AG history, the church had been ambivalent and suspicious about secular college and university education. Ashcroft's vision countered this mindset and motivated future positive attitudes and actions of the AG toward ministry to students attending the state colleges and universities. He planted seed that influenced the organizing of Chi Alpha (XA) in the next decade. The formal establishment of a national campus ministry program was at hand.

1950s Experiment
1,852 colleges and universities
2,281,298 college students
29,813 international students enrolled on U.S. campuses
From 0 to 34 Chartered Chi Alpha groups
U.S. population: 151,325,798

What happened in the 1950s?

The presidents in the 1950s were Harry Truman and Dwight Eisenhower. Prosperity, apple-pie values, the good old days; watching color TV began in 1951; conservative values; Korean War; segregation of public schools ended and integration began; Rosa Parks; Alaska and Hawaii become states; *USS Nautilus*, was the first nuclear submarine; rock'n roll emerged: Elvis Presley, Jerry Lee Lewis, Buddy Holly, Richie Valens, Bo Diddley, and Big Bopper. Crooners like Perry Como, Frank Sinatra, and Nat King Cole remained popular along with folk music like the Kingston Trio; beatniks; the launch of the interstate highway system; religion made a big resurgence (evangelist Billy Graham); the term teenager was used; "In God We Trust" on U.S. currency.

CHAPTER 2

Experiment 1950s

A Professor Organizes Chi Alpha (XA)

As the Assemblies of God grew and a higher proportion of American youth attended college, leaders realized that viable student ministries involving Pentecostal students needed to be developed and could have far-reaching potential on many campuses.

J. Calvin Holsinger studied history as an undergraduate at the University of Pittsburgh and later completed a doctorate at Temple University in Philadelphia. In 1948, at the age of 20, Holsinger accepted an invitation to teach history and speech and Central Bible Institute in Springfield, Missouri. As an undergraduate student at U Pitt, he was active in campus ministry. His student ministry experience and his study of the Reformation, plus history of revivals and awakenings on college campuses, inspired him to work with students. He knew college students have the capacity to impact the world, so in addition to his teaching responsibilities at CBI, he began teaching a college-age Sunday School class at nearby Central Assembly of God.

From here he and a handful of students launched a Bible study on the campus of Southwest Missouri State College (SMS). He knew having a presence on campus was the key to reaching students and establishing AG campus ministry.

College students learn new ideas and listen to new concepts. It is not just religion that is affected. It is politics. It is family life. Everything is affected. So, if somebody presents the gospel to students, they are willing to consider it.

Campus Ambassador Magazine

The *College Fellowship Bulletin* was renamed *Campus Ambassadors Magazine (CAM)* in 1952. *CAM* included articles on doctrine, apologetics, practical Christian living, and AG news. Holsinger became editor and wrote articles like "How to Begin a Chi Alpha Group."

Pastors Appoint a Chaplain for Chi Alpha

Local AG church leaders in Springfield knew there existed a need to provide spiritual support to students who attended nearby SMS and Drury College. In the fall of 1952, the pastors and presbyters from the Springfield section of the AG Southern Missouri District took deliberate steps to ensure viable, consistent ministry among AG college students. The pastors appointed Holsinger as chaplain. His assignment was to assist the district and nearby churches to start a local campus-based program for AG students in Springfield.

Origin of the Greek letters XA

Holsinger wanted the organizational name for AG campus ministry to be identifiable and acceptable to the AG constituency, appeal to college students, and communicate the ministry's purpose on campus. He saw value in using Greek letters that carried academic sophistication and tradition of Greek honor societies. In 1953, he proposed using the Greek letters XA (Chi Alpha) to represent the name for the AG collegiate ministry — 2 Corinthians 5:20:

We are therefore Christ's ambassadors, (Christou Apostoloi, Greek for Christ sent ones) as though God were making His appeal through us. We implore you on Christ's behalf: Be reconciled to God.

He wanted students to think of themselves as being *"sent"* to their university. Students agreed the Greek letters fit their collegiate atmosphere and adopted the Greek letters XA. Holsinger presented the objectives for XA using Luke 2:52: "And Jesus increased in wisdom and stature, and in favor with God and man." The objectives were emphasized as worship, training, service, and social.

Chi Alpha Becomes a Nationwide Ministry

The national CA Department took the next step to organize the XA campus ministry program nationwide by inviting Holsinger to serve part time as the first national campus adviser. He worked part time from 1954 to 1956 and led the initial development of XA nationwide. He outlined three national goals for college ministry:

1. To provide spiritual encouragement to students
2. To develop and suggest aids for better campus witness
3. To suggest ways that pastors in college communities could help AG students

There were 12 chartered XA groups the first academic year, and 18 the following school year.

First Chi Alpha Manual and Chaplains

Holsinger wrote the first *Chi Alpha Manual,* a 50-page loose-leaf notebook, in 1956. The manual explained the reasons for organizing a chapter, how to get started, and the program of a college CA group. The notebook noted, along with useful secular training, every college student should be instructed in spiritual matters. Holsinger wanted the students to recognize the importance of having a presence on campus. They can live a vibrant Christian life and witness for Christ, and as an organized group on campus they can be more effective.

The XA program included: (1) prayer gatherings, (2) study groups, (3) Christian social activity, and (4) service. The first *Chi Alpha Manual* was used for a decade.

Chaplains

In the early stages of XA, a local AG pastor was appointed to serve as a chaplain. Pastors made themselves available to the students as chaplains to provide spiritual guidance and oversight. These pastors/chaplains understood that their involvement in reaching out to college students would not necessarily translate into increased Sunday church attendance, additional workers in the church, or greater financial giving, but the investment was well worth it. One chaplain explained, "In spite of all the sacrifice of time and labor, shepherding a group of AG students is one of the most rewarding privileges you might ever have." Chaplains encouraged students to remain Pentecostal, instructed them to live spiritual lives, and to appreciate the role of the Church.

Legacy

Holsinger is credited for the vision and legacy of XA. He chose the organizational name, designed the program, wrote the first *Chi Alpha Manual,* and launched the AG campus ministry of XA nationwide.

William Menzies, a graduate of Wheaton College and former student president of the Wheaton College Assembly CA organization, the first known campus ministry for AG students prior to XA, became the second national XA campus adviser in the national CA Department in 1958. He worked part time as the campus adviser and editor of *CAM* while teaching at CBI. By spring 1959, there were 1,864 AG students representing 298 schools with 25 XA chapters. Menzies led XA until 1962.

The relatively stability of the 1950s and early 1960s would quickly change by the mid-1960s. The collegiate population would double and then begin to soar. Higher education was fast becoming essential to life and work in America.

Evolution 1960s
2,021 colleges and universities
4,145,065 college students
53,107 international students enrolled in U.S. campuses
From 31 to 98 chartered Chi Alpha groups
U.S. population: 179,323,175

What happened in the 1960s?

Dwight Eisenhower (1953-1961), John F. Kennedy (1961-1963), Lyndon Johnson (1963-1969), and Richard Nixon (1969-1974) were the presidents. Peace Corps, Cuban Missile Crisis, man walks on the moon (1969), JFK assassinated, a movement away from the conservative 1950s, resulting in revolutionary thinking and real change in the cultural fabric of American life; generation gap; the Age of Aquarius, reform and revolution; all the orthodoxies of government, church, and society called into question; youth denounced materialism and capitalism; the Beatles made their U.S. debut on *The Ed Sullivan Show* in 1964. More than 450,000 attended Woodstock in 1969; drug use (LSD and marijuana), sexual experimentation, the birth control pill, communal living and trying non-Western religions. College became centers of debate and scenes of protest; Vietnam War, Civil Rights movement, Martin Luther King Jr. was assassinated; National Organization for Women (NOW) questioned the unequal treatment of women addressing women's rights and the women's lib movement.

CHAPTER 3

Evolution 1960s

The cultural turmoil of the '60s

In the 1960s, society turned upside down. Every moral value that undergirded the social consensus came into question. Institutions like home, church, and government were called into question, and authority lost its credibility. Anti-establishment led to protests, boycotts, and bombings on campus. The cultural turmoil of the 1960s was pervasive on college campuses with Marxism, the sexual revolution, civil rights, and war protests.

Appointment of a national college youth representative

In 1962, there were three times as many AG students attending state colleges than those enrolled in AG Bible colleges. National XA reported 34 student-led XA chapters assisted by local AG pastors serving as chaplains. It was clear that the responsibilities of the college youth division had grown to such dimensions that a full-time college youth representative (CYR) was needed. Owen Carr of the national Christ's Ambassadors department observed the need for a full-time national CYR for XA and brought the need to the AG leadership. In January 1963, the AG Executive Presbytery granted permission to engage a full-time CYR. The first two CYRs only served one year, and the third for three years, and the fourth appointed in 1968 continued into the beginning of the 1970s. Having national representation was important, but turnover affected continuity and development.

Lee Shultz, the First Full-Time National CYR

Shultz became the national CYR in 1963 and served one year. He traveled extensively to promote and expand XA. In order to introduce and establish an officially recognized student organization on campus in the 1960s, Shultz met directly with a college president or dean. In August 1963, during the 30th General Council held in Memphis, Tennessee, Shultz conducted the first national XA meeting of a dozen pastors and students interested in campus ministry. During his tenure as CYR, the number of XA chartered groups increased from 34 to 41.

Russ Cox Named the Second National CYR

Cox took over June 1964. During his one-year tenure, he redesigned *CAM* by converting it to a pocket-sized, 32-page magazine, first published in the September/October 1964 issue. He led the second national XA gathering in Des Moines, Iowa, in August 1965, during the 31st General Council. The number of XA chapters increased from 41 to 51 during his tenure. He traveled and spoke at numerous XA retreats nationwide.

Rick Howard Became the Third National CYR

Howard began in 1965 and served three years. Howard was independent, dynamic, and persuasive. He had a keen mind and brought an enthusiastic vision to the development of college ministry. He envisioned XA not only as a campus ministry, but as a leadership training program for the AG, the Pentecostal movement in general, and the Christian world at large.

Howard was the representative during the early days of the

counterculture revolution of the 1960s. This era was an unsettling time when anti-authority and anti-establishment attitudes permeated the youth generation. It took a unique and gifted leader to steer XA through one of the most explosive times on campuses in America. For him, the instability on campuses provided opportunity to reach collegians searching for God's truth. He captured the zeitgeist of the 1960s and channeled an evangelistic fervor into the ministry to reach collegians for Christ.

He challenged Christian students to reject a "survival mentality" on campus. Howard explained: "Originally college ministry was founded on the premise that something should be done to maintain the faith of our own AG young people going off to college — admittedly a defensive posture." He changed the view of college ministry to include XA as an evangelistic "beachhead" on campus, a witness to the lordship of Christ, the reliability of scriptural revelation, and the indwelling presence of the Holy Spirit. He admonished XA groups meeting on campus to "be a cell of life where students gather to refresh themselves mentally, spiritually, and socially, and go to the campus and into dorms as dynamic personal witnesses for Christ in the power of the Holy Spirit."

Howard edited *CAM* from 1965 to 1968, providing a stimulating and relevant resource for college students. Issues like "Christian Debate Over the War" challenged readers to grapple with the divisiveness in society over involvement in the Vietnam War, the controversy over the draft, and protests on campus against the war. In the January 1967 issue, there was a story on the move of the Holy Spirit at the University of California-Berkeley campus, and the first XA Chi Alpha student center.

He wrote a new hardback version of the *Chi Alpha Manual* in 1966, which included the first written history of Chi Alpha, "The Story of the Assemblies of God College Ministry." XA groups doubled from

41 to 79 chapters. Howard updated the purpose of Chi Alpha:

1. Chi Alpha provides outreach to the often-neglected mission field of college and university campus through a dynamic beachhead of full-gospel students.

2. Chi Alpha promotes individual Christian maturity through worship, service, training, and fellowship.

3. Chi Alpha establishes continual dialogue between students and denomination, including the interpretation of the Assemblies of God agencies and ministries.

Jerry Sandidge was the Fourth National CYR

Sandidge was the fourth national and last CYR to be appointed in the 1960s. He began in 1968 and stepped down in 1970. Sandidge believed XA could be influential in both leadership development and the production of quality literature that addressed sensitive topics. He focused considerable energy on his writing abilities into editing *CAM* from 1968 to 1971. *CAM* addressed issues of civil disobedience, social concerns, sex on campus, reaching Muslims, and Christian debate over the Vietnam War.

Sandidge became concerned with the Western European culture and the dearth of Christian witness on the campuses. He traveled for five weeks and visited 12 countries to survey Pentecostal ministry to students on European campuses. He returned with a deep burden for European collegians without a Pentecostal witness, and eventually he was approved as the first world missionary to pioneer university ministry in Europe.

Retreats

The first weekend statewide and multistate retreats began in the 1960s and continue today, and are integral in creating an identity for XA. Often planned by the district CA presidents and student leaders, students from XA groups and church groups gathered at camps to hear a speaker, enjoy fellowship, and worship. The national CYR was often invited as a guest speaker along with AG pastors and educators. Students from different campuses were eager to meet with one another for fellowship, worship, and training. The XA groups were small and a retreat gave students a larger view of campus ministry.

District XA Leadership

The local campus minister position did not exist in the 1960s. The District CA President (D-CAP), now District Youth Director (DYD), was responsible for XA development, but most of their responsibilities were directed toward the district and local AG church youth programming. The DYD resourced CA groups and spoke in local churches, as well as sectional and district youth gatherings. Because most of the ministry of XA operated outside the church and on campus, the need for more hands-on local campus leadership was needed.

As XA grew, the DYD with a plate full of youth ministry responsibilities could not fully devote time to XA. By the late 1960s, a few districts acted to endorse either a part-time district XA representative (D-XAR) or a full-time district XA director (D-XAD). The XA district representative or director could promote XA, connect with university students on campus, start campus groups, link churches to XA and sponsor retreats. Between 1967 and 1969 Minnesota, New York/New Jersey, Michigan, and Wisconsin/Northern Michigan were the first four districts to appoint district XA leaders. The national CYR position was vacant for seven months before a new and fifth CYR was appointed in 1971.

In the next decade, the collegiate population experienced rapid growth, changes in the collegiate culture accelerated, and the role of the campus minister began to emerge. All of this demonstrated a critical need for greater oversight and continuity in national leadership.

What happened in the 1970s?

Richard Nixon resigns under threat of impeachment. Gerald Ford and Jimmy Carter also were U.S. presidents in the 1970s. Sears Tower (now Willis Tower) in Chicago is the tallest building in the world. America is defeated in Vietnam War. The last Americans (10 U.S. Marines) depart from Vietnam on April 30, 1975; the leaked Pentagon Papers discredited the Vietnam War policies of the Johnson and Nixon administrations. Four students were killed and nine injured when National Guardsmen opened fire during an anti-war demonstration at Kent State University. The generational name "Baby Boomer" was used for the first time in 1970. Women, minorities, and gays increasingly demanded full legal equality and privileges in society. OPEC Arab oil embargo caused shortage of fuel and energy prices skyrocketed. Recession. *Roe v. Wade* legalizes abortion. American bicentennial celebrated. Affirmative action became a controversial policy; radioactive leak at Three Mile Island nuclear plant; Iranian militant students seize the U.S. embassy in Tehran with 66 hostages for 444 days.

CHAPTER 4

Examination 1970s

The Jesus People Movement and Charismatic Renewal

The Jesus People Movement was a spiritual revival among the youth counterculture that began on the West Coast. The Charismatic Renewal started when an Episcopalian rector from California was baptized in the Holy Spirit and wrote *The Holy Spirit and You.* Catholic professors and students from Duquesne University in Pittsburgh and the University of Notre Dame in Indiana experienced the baptism of the Holy Spirit, and the renewal swept across the nation. Jesus People showed up en masse on the doorsteps of churches and campuses, and charismatics who had experienced the gift of the Spirit began to gather at retreats, large events, and in special services in their churches. Many of the early leaders in the Jesus People Movement were Pentecostal evangelists and pastors. The movement and renewal challenged AG churches to respond. Local XA groups embraced Jesus People and the move of the Holy Spirit among Pentecostals and charismatics. Their new worship music and songs were a departure from typical church music that featured organ and piano. Instead, came a vibrant worship style with acoustic guitar, much adoration of God, and the move of the Holy Spirit. The teaching on the gifts of the Holy Spirit and the priesthood of believers called for every member (student) in the group to participate in the body of Christ.

Articles published in the AG publication the *Pentecostal Evangel (PE)* revealed how AG churches were reticent to swap the 1950s Christ's Ambassador youth meetings and the early 1960s jargon of "youth rallies" with the Jesus People Movement idioms like "Bible raps" and "Jesus festivals." Some conversion accounts emphasized hippies getting a haircut and a bath, implying that a credible salvation experience must also comprise an abstention from the counterculture. Pictures show AG ministers awkwardly placed in coffeehouses and outdoor meetings with crewcuts, horn-rimmed glasses, and suits and ties alongside young Jesus People with long hair, jeans, and T-shirts. Editorials in the *PE* reflect a full range of opinions from supportive to prophetic warnings. In contrast, however, many small-town newspapers, some books, and the *PE* are peppered with stories of AG churches and evangelistic organizations that reached out to the hippies and experienced transformation and numerical growth. Thomas E. Trask, future AG superintendent, acknowledged churches that welcomed the Jesus People had the joy of seeing great harvest, though some were divided in their opinions.

Fifth National College Youth Representative

In 1971, XA, after being directed by four different national CYRs in eight years, gained much-needed continuity through the leadership of the fifth national CYR, C. David Gable. He would serve for eight years, introducing programming that solidified XA for the 1970s and beyond. Gable had a relaxed, casual leadership style. He emphasized authentic, unpretentious relationships and evidenced an inclusive spirit that welcomed different styles and approaches to leadership and ministry. He brought insight into understanding the role of XA and the university campus to AG district and executive leaders. He endeared himself to students and those working on campuses.

Gable described the 1970s as "a seminal period for youth action of all sorts. Life, apparel, worldview, and ministry all changed rapidly. . . young people who put down everything else to make Jesus first, publicly, in all aspects of life. It's not just long-hairs putting down drugs, promiscuity, and the occult, but also the neat, well-groomed kids coming off ego trips and prideful church games to follow Christ."

First SALT (Student Activists Leadership Training)

One of the first programs Gable introduced in 1972 was the regional SALT conference. It was held in the South Central region at the Southwestern Assemblies of God College in Waxahachie, Texas, from June 1 to 10. The approach was to get campus activists to light a fire of vision, and secondly, get some white-haired old genius, some old academician to keep us intellectually respectable and teach the Bible, but do it in a way so that students from secular colleges who knew good scholarship could get into the text and see the intellectual respectability of their faith. There were 23 in attendance at the first SALT. Other significant components of SALT were dynamic worship, workshops on implementing campus ministry, and the integration of faith with various academic disciplines, and small groups called *allelous* (uh-lay-loose), the Greek word for "one another," derived from the Greek word *koinonia.*

With the onset of the 1970s, Gable noted that activity had settled on the campuses and there were no dominant trends. He observed this as a reaction to several things: "the failure of the youth revolt of the '60s to achieve any major change in society; disillusionment with rainbow-chasing drug experiences; and dissatisfaction with the answers humanistic philosophies had been giving for too long." He emphatically claimed, "This reflective mood is fantastically fertile ground for God's answer in Christ to be sounded."

By 1974, SALT conferences were held in six regions. The largest was SC at the University of Oklahoma in Norman, with more than 400 in attendance. In addition to regional SALT, six national SALTs convened in 1975 and 1977, and four times during the next decade, bringing students and staff together nationwide.

Full-Time District Chi Alpha Directors (D-XADs)

Gable reported six district XA leaders when he came to the national office in the fall of 1971. They were district (state, combination of states, or several geographic areas within a state) level leaders that would help XA develop. Eight more D-XADs were appointed by districts within the next five years. Gable directed the second national DXAD seminar in 1972 with 21 in attendance. The following year, attendance doubled with 42 full- and part-time D-XADs, district youth directors, and a few local campus ministers. According to Gable, the district representatives were a mixed bag. Districts would designate a pastor, perhaps from a college town, who was presumed to have an affinity for campus ministry. In some cases that really was genuine. In other cases, it just wasn't happening. Throughout the 1970s, a good number of DYDs and several D-XADs had significant influence on XA starting local XA groups and organizing retreats.

Full-Time Vocational Campus Ministers

In the early to mid-1970s, under Gable's leadership, the position of "the local campus minister" came to fruition and would become a viable ministry vocation in the AG. The October 1974 *CAM* recorded an early account of personnel serving nationwide. Gable included photographs of 24 local campus ministers with a brief description of their XA activity. By 1979, 50 full-time campus ministers served in XA.

First Institute of Campus Ministry (ICM)

The Jesus People Movement and Charismatic Renewal raised up countless students and leaders who wanted to love and serve Jesus. Young men and women were called to campus ministry, but there had been no formal campus ministry staff training for XA until the mid-1970s. Students who found Christ on campus and had been called to lead university ministry often lacked Bible training. Students graduating from AG colleges with training in biblical studies and theology often lacked experience on secular campuses. Few campus workers had ministerial credentials or training beyond student Bible studies, prayer meetings, worship gatherings, and fellowship in the local XA group. Most had no idea why they would need ministerial credentials to lead campus ministry. That all changed with annual training being offered.

Gable saw the need to channel and conserve what God was doing on campus and to provide specific training for those desiring to serve campus ministry. In 1976, Gable launched the annual Institute of Campus Ministry (ICM) at the AG Graduate School (now Assemblies of God Theological Seminary at Evangel University). It became the most important educational training for XA staff then and today. Ten attended the first ICM. This training was designed primarily for preparing XA campus missionaries. By 1979, the ICM curriculum for training had expanded beyond the typical seminary class lecture format to a 10-day full participation requirement: living on campus, meals together, small groups, worship, prayer, extended class lectures and interactive sessions. The 1978 ICM had 25 students in attendance and the 1979 ICM had 29.

Campus Ministers Seminar

After conducting seven national seminars for district XA leaders, in 1977 Gable changed the D-XAD Seminar name to the Campus Ministers Seminar (forerunner of the Campus Ministers

Conference) and shifted the primary focus to train and provide resources to the current local XA campus ministers that continued to increase in number. Eighty-six men and women from across the country attended the March 13–16, 1977, gathering. Two-thirds of the attendees led campus ministry on a local campus. The others were district leadership for XA.

In 1979, a total of 106 men and women attended the conference. National XA leadership invited national specialists from sister campus ministry organizations Young Life, Youth for Christ, and Barnabas Inc. to address the group.

XA Ministry Principles and Philosophy

At the 1977 Campus Ministers Seminar in Springfield, campus leaders selected six XA personnel to meet with Gable to develop a present-day philosophy to unify campus ministry across the nation. The committee was comprised of the national CYR, two D-XADs, two campus ministers, and two pastors of campus churches. The committee met from May 28 to June 1, 1977, in San Antonio, Texas. Gable chaired the group, referred affectionately as the "San Antonio Seven." It created a concise set of ministry principles for XA. The work was edited, submitted to all campus ministers and DYDs for input, and finalized as the "The Original Chi Alpha Philosophy in 1977."

The Chi Alpha Fourfold Philosophy (1977)

The strategy and approach for establishing campus ministry was based on Acts 2:42–47. This passage describes a Spirit-filled group or "community" of believers who worship God, pray together, rejoice in one another's company, teach and study the Word of God, and tell others about Jesus Christ. XA realized the most effective apologetic for establishing campus ministry was the coming together as a group on campus for biblically commanded activity.

XA uses the phrase "gathered people of God on campus" (community) to stress the position that we can be more visible and effective as a (Christian) group rather than isolated individuals. Biblical community is the essential component of faith and development and witness to the world. XA, as a faith community established on campus, is the vehicle God uses to bring students to faith and maturity in Jesus Christ. The philosophy emphasized four key components of the XA community on campus.

Worship, Fellowship, Discipleship, Witness

The fourfold philosophy unified and distinguished XA from disparate approaches of campus groups nationwide. It became the foundation and framework for the future. It defined XA beliefs, how it functioned, and served as the standard by which existing and new groups measured and evaluated themselves. Gable described the importance of this integrated model of ministry:

> Without good worship, we end up a merely human club or society, powerless and dry. Without deep, honest fellowship, we are less than the family of God; lonely with social needs unmet, co-fighters, co-workers, but not brethren. Without discipleship that forms us and keeps us growing, we are stale and dull, mediocre and irrelevant, with the Word compartmentalized and unapplied. Without a heart for evangelism, we are ingrown, incestuous and sterile.

XA leaders actively owned the philosophy and immediately implemented it on campus. In 1978, the second ICM training curriculum formally integrated the new XA fourfold philosophy. The philosophy guided the curriculum and centered on the biblical basis and practical implementation of being a community on campus of worship, fellowship, discipleship, and witness.

End of an Era

The fourfold philosophy was Gable's most important legacy to XA development. It set in motion the core principles of XA and continues as the structure for the ministry today. He successfully brought together an assortment of leaders who rallied around the ideals of XA and eagerly sought to apply those principles to campus ministry. He harnessed the fruitfulness and power of regional and national SALTs to develop a strong XA identity nationwide and on campus. He introduced ICM in 1976 to train campus ministers and was instrumental in advancing the role of the local campus minister.

The first head count of students who participated in XA on campuses across the nation was reported by Gable in the February 1978 *CAM*. The report recorded almost 6,000 students in attendance for main weekly gatherings and slightly over 9,000 representing the broader number of students participating in all XA events on campus. He listed 155 groups for 1977 with an average attendance of 29. In 1978, a total of 195 groups were listed with an average of 30 in attendance. In 1979, 63% of groups remained student-led. A small number of groups had 60 to 75 students.

What had we learned about reaching students for Christ? First, the rise of full-time campus ministers as the most effective means for reaching students. Second, codifying and implementing a current XA philosophy on ministry. Third, the introduction of regional and national conferences and training venues for students and staff. All of these contributed to creating an XA culture and increased effectiveness on campus.

Excellence 1980s
3,321 colleges and universities
12,096,985 college students
311,882 international students enrolled in U.S. campuses
From 182 reduced to 166 chartered Chi Alpha groups
U.S. population: 226,542,199

What happened in the 1980s?

Jimmy Carter, Ronald Reagan, and George H. W. Bush were presidents in the 1980s. Iran hostages released. AIDs. Space shuttle Challenger explosion. John Lennon (member of the Beatles) murdered outside a hotel in New York City in 1980. U.S. Olympic Committee voted to boycott the Summer Olympics in Moscow in response to the Soviet Union invasion of Afghanistan in 1980. Prince Charles and Lady Diana marry at Westminster Abbey in 1981. Apple launches its MacIntosh computer in 1984. Cold War ends with fall of the Berlin Wall in 1989. The Soviet Empire is dismantled. U.S. bombs Libya. Invasion of Panama. Financial panic. Rambo I, II, and III.

CHAPTER 5

Excellence 1980s

The National College Youth Training Coordinator

The increasing requests for national office services and resources led to the creation of a second national XA position, the college youth training coordinator. Dennis Gaylor, the South Texas District XA director, was invited to come to the national office and work with Dave Gable, the national college youth rep. Dennis would edit *CAM* and a *XA Newsletter*, develop training and communication tools, and assist with administration. Dennis was outgoing, positive and approachable, creative, and big-picture minded with a view to the long term.

Sixth National XA Leader

Only four months until the beginning of the 1980s, Gable stepped down from his national position. Gaylor would take the reins of national XA as the sixth national leader. He would build on the momentum of the 1970s with SALT conferences and staff training programs underway, the emergence of the campus minister position, and the fourfold philosophy of ministry applied at the local level.

XA Launched AG High School Ministry

Ongoing study had been underway to establish a parallel AG campus ministry for high school students led by Jim McCorkle, the national youth department AIM rep, and later national secretary. The NYD were testing out the fourfold XA philosophy adapted for high school youth referred to as Re-Acts. There was nascent activity in high school ministry led by youth pastors in Sherman, Texas; Tacoma, Washington; and Carlinville, Illinois. Youth Alive high school ministry was introduced and launched at the district youth directors conference in February 1979 and in August at the 38th General Council in Baltimore. Dave Gable wrote a *Hi-Teen Sunday School Fall Quarterly* entitled "Reaching Your High School Campus for Christ."

There have been 10 Youth Alive (YA) directors operating out of the national youth department since 1979, and a campus missions coordinator serving in AG U.S. Missions. The coordinator oversees the appointment of full-time YA missionaries and associates. In 2023, there are 30 YA missionaries and spouses, four district coordinators, 12 missionary associates and spouses and four career associates and spouses.

Following General Council, Gable stepped down and transitioned to become a pastor in California. Instead of replacing the second XA position, the priority shifted to accommodate the nascent YA program. The college youth rep and training coordinator's positions would be combined into the national college ministry specialist position, and a high school ministry specialist was added that fall to head up and develop YA. In the years ahead, YA would develop as a preeminent middle and high school campus ministry with resources, conferences, personnel, and student-led clubs on and off campuses. The YA program would remain in the NYD with nationally appointed YA missionaries coordinated through AG U.S.

Missions. Today the director of student discipleship in the NYD provides leadership to YA.

The Role of the Campus Minister Here to Stay

By the 1980s, XA was active on 175 campuses throughout the nation. Campus leadership unified around the fourfold philosophy of worship, fellowship, discipleship, and witness introduced in 1977. This engagement ensured balance, stability, and excellence in the ministry. The role of a campus minister was here to stay in that it had become a part of the landscape with more XA groups led by qualified staff persons.

Annual chartering groups and affiliating campus leaders were a priority in order to determine the state of XA, and the extent of XA. The collected data provided accurate information to improve decision making, allocation of resources, and strategic planning. As XA identified cooperating campus groups and affiliated leaders that affirmed vision and mission, XA ministry became more unified and matured.

During the decade, XA ministry was overseeing the increasing number of campus ministers in the field, conducting training for new and current campus ministers, publishing a magazine and training materials, planning and executing national conferences, encouraging and assisting with evangelistic outreach and collegiate missions teams abroad, resourcing the nascent international student ministry, officially chartering groups and affiliating leaders, managing a budget, and promoting XA at every level and in different venues.

Training Leadership — ICM and CMC

Training new and current leaders continued through the vehicles of ICM started in 1976, and CMC begun in 1977. New campus ministers received uniform training taught by existing campus ministers with experience ministering to students, representing different leadership styles, campus groups, and parts of the country. In 1982, the *Campus Leaders Notebook: Essentials for Campus Ministry* was published. It integrated the fourfold XA philosophy and outlined operating principles for XA. Every XA campus leader received a complimentary copy, and it was the text for ICM and campus ministry. The notebook would serve XA for the next two decades.

CMC provided annual gatherings for all current XA personnel to challenge and resource them for the ministry they were doing on campuses. Most groups were led by campus ministers, raised up in a local XA group, and remaining after graduation to bring good news to students in the same way they had experienced Christ as students.

Campus Missionary-in-Training Programs

The first XA internship was in 1977 held at one campus, Western Washington University. By the mid-1980s, a nationally recognized campus ministry internship program was established. Nine- to 10-month staff training programs that met certain standards were officially recognized as the national Campus Missionary-in-Training (CMIT) programs. By the end of the 1980s, there were eight approved CMITs in several locations nationwide.

Regional Representatives

In 1983, nine regional representatives were appointed to oversee the development of XA in each district and to plan the regional SALT and assist the national director. They typically were local campus ministers or district leaders who would volunteer in the regional role. Representatives brought together each year campus staff for fellowship and training and planning. The reps met annually with the national XA leader, reported on what was developing, and coordinated planning for XA nationwide.

Regional and National SALTs

Throughout the 1980s, regional and national SALTs, XA's foremost student training, continued to equip and mobilize students for ministry on campus seeding new XA groups and leaders. Four national SALTs were conducted every three years in the 1980s, bringing together a wider representation of students nationwide, and accomplishing more as a nationwide gathering instead of regional meetings. The annual regional and national SALTs provided a place where students and staff gathered, creating unity, establishing a unique campus ministry culture, and a growing a student movement. At the 1989 national SALT, XA launched "the national wave of prayer," challenging XA groups to set aside Thursdays for specific and united prayer "waves" across America's campuses during the noon hour. It was very successful, with 400 prayer groups representing 2,300 students engaged each Thursday in the national wave of prayer.

International Students

A ministry to the emergent numbers of international students coming to the U.S. to study on America's colleges and universities demanded XA begin a concerted effort to launch an international student ministry. Interested personnel working with internationals began to connect and resource one another. A handful of AG churches and several XA campus groups started reaching out to internationals. *A Manual of Ministry to Internationals* was published by XA in 1983, and training was incorporated into XA training venues. A stand-alone conference for workers ministering to international students was introduced in 1988.

Major Restructuring: XA Becomes a Department in Missions

Halfway through the 1980s, XA would experience a watershed moment that would set the trajectory of XA for decades to come. As XA matured, leadership wrestled with giving greater definition to XA, and determining where it fits in the AG organization to realize its potential. XA had been in the national youth department since it formally began in the 1950s. In many ways being aligned with the youth department in church ministries was incomplete as youth ministry was church-centric, and XA was operating on the secular campus outside the four walls of the local church, with so much of the ministry on campus occurring during weekdays.

Gaylor, the sixth national leader, submitted a proposal that outlined rationales for study that included:

- Revise organizational structure to facilitate growth and expansion of personnel and programming.
- Establish XA's identity as missions.
- Collaborate with AG World Missions and AG U.S. Missions.
- Expand training to accommodate current and future growth.
- Develop international student ministry.
- Partner with other national campus ministries.
- Initiate financial development and advancement.
- Promote XA within Christian higher education and church ministries.
- Examine need for additional resident leadership positions in national XA.

Seismic Change

The historic study involved two representatives from AGWM, AGUSM, Church Ministries (national youth department), and the Spiritual Life/Evangelism coordinator as chair. The assistant general superintendent joined the committee. The study and conclusion resulted in seismic change moving XA from the national youth department in church ministries to become the college ministries department located in AG U.S. Missions. As one committee member stated, "This is not merely a cosmetic change or a game of musical chairs. This is a game changer that blew the ceiling off of XA for years to come." This would be approved by the General Council in 1987, resulting in XA physically relocating from the youth department and setting up new offices and becoming a department itself in U.S. Missions. The national XA leader's position would be elevated to national director.

This was a monumental change, identifying XA with missions and with the understanding that missions practices, methodologies, and strategies would be applied in the new department. It would take the remaining years of the 1980s for the AG church to be educated and embrace the change (XA as missions), and accept the campus missionary position. The specialized campus missionary was different from church staff positions in that it was cross-cultural and the church functioned around Sundays and a weeknight, whereas campus ministry operated during the week with events on the weekends. The church calendar and academic calendar required flexibility so campus ministry fit the students' needs and schedules, often different from the church calendar and its programming. Discipleship of university students took a quantum leap in the 1980s.

Established 1990s

3,559 colleges and universities

13,818,637 college students

407,529 international students enrolled in U.S. campuses

From 186 to 206 chartered Chi Alpha groups

U.S. population: 248,178,302

What happened in the 1990s?

George W. Bush and Bill Clinton were presidents in the 1990s. Iraq army invades Kuwait in 1990 and a U.S. led coalition attacked Iraq's army in 1991 and liberated Kuwait. Gulf War, Oklahoma City terrorist bombing; World Trade Center bombing, Bill Clinton the first "Boomer" president; Google; Y2K, Diana princess of Wales dies in Paris car crash; 51-day standoff in Waco, Texas, begins when ATF agents attempt to arrest Branch Davidian leader David Koresh. Stephen King, John Grisham, and Danielle Steel are bestselling authors in 1992. In 1998, at age 77, John Glenn became the oldest astronaut in space.

CHAPTER 6

Established 1990s

XA was elevated to department status to AG U.S. Missions three years prior to the 1990s. This organizational restructuring was consequential and positioned XA for greater effectiveness and influence in the years ahead.

In the first year of the new decade, a Campus Ministry Consultation (informally called the Arizona 38 based on the number of leaders who participated and the location) convened. Ten strategies were outlined for the 1990s:

> 1. Prayer was added to the original XA fourfold philosophy and was introduced and emphasized with the national wave of prayer (campus groups gathering at the noon hour each Thursday to pray).
> 2. The first residential national staff became a reality.
> 3. The national missionary appointment approval process solidified in the 1990s enhanced recruitment, training, and placing campus missionaries.
> 4. Missionary personal support raising training was introduced.

5. International student ministry continues as an unparalleled opportunity for world missions stateside.

6. By mid-1990s, the conference for district leaders became a stand-alone event, and was conducted annually to equip current and new XA district leaders.

7. Devise strategic targeting and planting new XA groups as more campus ministers received national missionary appointment. The approach of sending teams rather than a single individual or couple to plant new groups became the established practice.

8. Every campus leader was challenged to tell the XA story, and promote a vision for campus ministry. Telling the XA story nationwide became more prominent.

9. Develop new outreach to students and expand student leadership training. The Student Institute of Campus Ministry was introduced in 1993 and held in one location. It would expand to five regions in the decades that followed.

10. Have students from every campus engaged in missions beyond the campus during their campus experience.

Updated vision and missions statements

Three years after these strategies were outlined and initiated, national leadership agreed it was time to get away to take a new look at the overall status of XA nationwide. It had been 16 years (1977) since the fourfold philosophy was introduced and embraced by all of XA. Campus leadership had implemented the biblical principles of worship, fellowship, discipleship, and witness at the local level during the 1980s, improving quality of ministry, stability, and continuity. The concept of being fully XA brought students and staff together, establishing a national identity and culture, and an understanding that local XA was part of something larger than themselves.

The Name Chi Alpha (XA)

By the 1990s, a number of campus groups chartered with XA had adopted other names for their local group, like University Christian Fellowship, Christians in Action, and Students for Christ. Many expressed concerns that we needed to maintain a unifying name for XA's identify and visibility. In 1992 at the Campus Ministers Conference, the national name Chi Alpha was debated and ultimately affirmed as the organizational name to remain. XA challenged every group to adopt the name XA. The benefits of everyone using the XA name were spelled out:

- One name unifies XA nationally
- Students can more easily find XA on any campus if one name is used
- A shared name enhances local and nationwide visibility and promotion
- A recognized national name and organization makes XA more attractive to donors and businesses
- One name allows XA to establish quality and unity among officially chartered groups, and protect the name.

It was understood that changing a name would create major disruption and expense, so "keep the name XA" was the decision, and unquestionably XA has greatly benefited from the use of one name during the past 30 years. XA does have a culture and a brand, and is recognized by other national campus organizations and churches.

Reconciling Students to Christ

In 1993, seven national XA leaders met in the Colorado Rockies at a mountain cabin to seek a fresh vision and mission for XA. Three days were spent rearticulating the essential values of XA and defining what XA should look like in the 21st century. The leaders envisioned objectives that would guide the vision and mission.

The motto and vision statement "Reconciling Students to Christ, transforming the university, the marketplace, and the world" was introduced. The vision would guide decisions, leadership practices, and community life. Six values: community, creativity, diversity, excellence, integrity, and servant leadership, would be expressed in living out the vision.

XA is Missions

The move of XA from the national youth department to become a college ministries department in missions, may be the most significant change since XA started in the 1950s. The identification with missions and the appointment of missionary personnel would solidify in the 1990s and open new opportunities for ministry and expansion. This change was major. This move recognized XA as missions and the university campus as a mission field, increased credibility for the role of a campus missionary, ensured further development with the new status as a department, and positioned XA to become a national campus ministry movement. XA had evolved from a loosely knit disparate band of campus workers scattered across the nation in the in 1980s to a solid group of trained and qualified campus missionaries in the 1990s.

First Resident National Leadership Team

The 1990s saw the first national field rep and resident staff team added to national XA. XA had operated for 27 years with only one national leader and one administrative secretary. Planning national conferences, writing and editing college publications, and representing XA in numerous venues was a full assignment. The most important responsibility was being entrusted with guarding the values, philosophy, and culture of XA. Expectations and pressures were high as XA had experienced growth and development and was now active in most states. XA was overseeing 200 chartered groups and 300 staff with an involvement of 8,000 students. As the organization grew, demands on leadership increased. XA was a national organization resourcing campus ministers in the field, providing specialized training, conducting regional student conferences, developing a ministry to international students, sponsoring student missions teams abroad, facilitating the starting of new campus groups, and communicating a vision for the campus.

Having a resident national staff team living in Springfield, Missouri, to strengthen the ability to serve a growing XA constituency, became a reality. The first national field rep served with the national director on the eve of the 1990s and until 1992. In 1992, the first resident national staff team of nationally appointed missionaries joined national XA operating out of the national office. Eight missionaries joined the national office between 1992 and 1999 to fill staff positions.

Charles Hackett, executive director of AGUSM, approved XA to physically relocate from AG headquarters in 1992 and rent offices in downtown Springfield to accommodate adding staff and XA growth. National XA relocated to the Woodruff Building (now Sky Eleven) in downtown Springfield that had the space needed. XA operated for eight years in that location, and relocated again in 2000 to an off-site building owned by AG U.S. Missions on the west side of the city. In all, XA operated off-site for 17 years until space was made available 2009 in the AG headquarters for XA to return.

National Missionary Appointment

Prior to the 1990s, there was no uniform system in place for personnel in XA to be funded or gain access to a national system to fulfill their call to campus ministry. Nationally appointed campus missionaries are required to have a national account and raise their ministry and work budgets. Most campus workers had accounts through a district, church, or personal account, or else had other employment, their spouse's employment, or volunteered. When XA introduced national missionary appointment for local XA campus ministers in 1992, it provided access to a national account and opportunity to itinerate in churches and among friends and family to raise a missionary personal and a work budget.

The AG structure for support was primarily itineration among churches in the respective districts. Other U.S. missionaries and world missionaries were raising support at the same time to get to their assignment, so to shorten the itineration time (average of 18 months to two years) in most contexts XA focused on individual donor support. XA communicated the vision for university ministry to students and alumni who benefited from XA, to parents and grandparents concerned for their college youth, and businesses that desired to invest in campus ministry as a way of investing in future leadership.

Around 60% of XA missionaries support came from individual donors with 40% from churches. Because XA was the AG ministry to the colleges and universities in the U.S., churches contributed to the XA ministry at the local level and made faith promises to the nationally appointed XA missionaries. For national missionary appointment among XA personnel to be understood and accepted, and for XA personnel to shift to national appointment, took time. The AG understands missions, so XA being aligned with missions soon gave credibility to campus ministry. The national appointment of local campus missionaries positioned XA long term for the future.

Institute of Campus Ministry and CMIT

The ICM and CMIT training venues begun in 1976 and 1977 coupled with national missionary appointment translated to more qualified personnel, increased longevity, and establishment of more campus ministries. In 1992, XA appointed its first 18 campus missionaries representing six districts and, by 1999, there were 213 appointed missionaries representing more than 30 districts.

Entry Level for New Campus Ministers

Not all campus workers were qualified or needed national appointment, but so many young men and women wanted to remain after graduation to be involved in campus ministry. An entry-level way for these men and women, many recent college graduates who had been involved in XA as undergraduates, to do campus ministry was the introduction of a new personnel category originating in 1997: the campus missionary associate (MA). Most of these MAs in the beginning were short-term and part-time campus workers, however, many remained in the MA role for five or 10 or more years serving as campus ministers typically with the campus director. They were not required to raise as large a budget as nationally appointed missionaries, and did not have all the benefits of national appointment. Interestingly, many MAs pursued national appointment after serving several years, or when they married and needed to increase their budgets. That first year there were 12 MAs and by the end of the 1990s there were 50 MAs. Interest in becoming a MA grew exponentially.

Campus Ministers Conference

The CMC occurred every year in the 1990s as the venue to build XA culture and equip leaders. Vison, identity, and unity were created as campus missionaries met together each year. The first CMIT Directors Seminar was held at the 1992 CMC. In 1996, XA had a bilingual CMC. National XA invited campus leaders from Latin American countries to CMC. In 1997, XA hosted its first family camp in Winter Park, Colorado, instead of CMC to encourage XA family participation. Programming for children was included with great success. All future CMCs would be designed to better serve families with programming for children and teens, lots of infant care, and discounted and comfortable accommodations to make it attractive for all to participate. In 1999, XA conducted six regional Leadership Summits in place of a one-location CMC to engage more personnel by making the training more accessible.

XA was strengthening nationwide with the new vision statement, resident national staff, training programs, national appointment, staff and student gatherings, and more interests and opportunities in stateside and world missions. The decade was marked by a sustained positive momentum for XA's growth and development.

Efficacious 2000s
4,084 colleges and universities
15,312,289 college students
547,867 international students enrolled in U.S. campuses
From 209 to 278 chartered Chi Alpha groups
2000 U.S. population: 281,424,603

What happened in the 2000s?

George W. Bush served as president from 2001-2009. Barack Obama (2009-2017) was the first Black president. This was a new millennium, beginning of a new century, the 21st. Hurricane Katrina in Louisiana 2005 was the costliest hurricane in U.S. history. On 9-11-2001, terrorists hijack airplanes and crash into the World Trade Center in New York City, the Pentagon, and a field near Shanksville, Pennsylvania. Iraq and Afghanistan Wars begin. Wikipedia launches in 2001, Apple iPod in 2001, Facebook in 2004, Apple iPod mini in 2004 and YouTube in 2009. Dot.com technology bubble. In 2004 largest earthquake ever recorded (9.3 magnitude) creates a tsunami devastating South Asia and 230,000 died. Space Shuttle Columbia breaks apart in reentry, killing seven astronauts on board. The first Harry Potter series published. SpongeBob SquarePants; virtual money: digital money, electric money, and Bitcoin.

CHAPTER 7

Efficacious 2000s

The 21st Century

By 2000, Dennis Gaylor, the sixth national director, had served in the national ministry for more than two decades, leading XA to a place of wide-ranging influence. The executive director of AGUSM, Charles Hackett, made a presentation in January 2000 to the AG Executive Presbytery, the decision-making body of the AG. He asserted the major role XA played on the secular campus to bring students to Christ. He reported that XA had competent leaders, detailed strategy, in-depth training, adequate finances, and a dependence on the supernatural.

With the onset of the year 2000, XA had come of age as a national campus ministry movement on 209 colleges and universities of America, involving 18,981 students in weekly gatherings. XA established a rhythm of recruiting, training, and assisting in the placement of men and women called to campus ministry.

Missionary appointment changed everything. XA went from a disparate handful of minimally funded and inadequately trained campus workers in the 1970s and 1980s with minimal credibility, to a large and effective national campus ministry movement with hundreds of well-trained staff and mature campus ministries by the

2000s. Ensuring that XA personnel can fulfill a call and career in campus ministry is crucial with entry into the 21st century.

The World SALT

A major event that set a trajectory for XA in the 21st century was the World SALT, a collegiate conference sponsored by XA USA. It convened in Los Angeles during the Christmas-New Year's break, 2000-2001. Students and campus ministers from across the U.S. and world missionaries and nationals from 49 countries representing 2,063 attendees from 250 campuses stateside and worldwide participated. The World SALT underscored that university ministry in the AG had come of age globally, and was a movement.

Commission on University Ministry

At the conclusion of the World SALT, a meeting convened involving 37 AG missionaries and leaders from 17 nations to discuss and report on university ministry activity around the globe, and ultimately asking, "What is God saying to us now in the 21st century about reaching university campuses with the gospel?" This led AGWM to form the Commission on University Ministry represented by AG world missionaries with university ministry assignments and regional directors serving throughout the world and U.S. XA national leadership. This was a significant step forward in mobilizing XA students and staff in world missions, and catalytic in the appointment of world missionaries to work with university students overseas. The commission would impart vision, develop strategies, and network to implement campus ministry globally. This commission travels each year to a different country to train and work with world missionaries and nationals active in university ministry. Their travel took them to Asia, Eurasia, Europe, Africa, and South America. The commission inspired by the World SALT would move XA to a new level and partnership with AGWM mobilizing students for mission unlike any previous time.

Missions Defined in the Fivefold Philosophy

"Reconciling students to Christ, transforming the university, the marketplace, and the world" originated from a national XA staff retreat in 1993 in Colorado, and gained traction in the new century. Recognizing the impact XA has beyond the campus into the marketplace and world gave impetus to consider what must be done locally and nationally to achieve effectiveness long term by what transpires on the university campus today.

The term "mission" replaced "witness" in the fivefold XA philosophy in 2006 to bring a greater understanding to the Great Commission and the implications for XA consistent with our vision statement on "reconciling the world." Establishing Spirit-empowered communities on campus that model worship, prayer, fellowship, discipleship, and mission is imperative.

What could Chi Alpha look like in the new century?

XA identified six values to guide ministry decisions, leadership practices, and community life. They are: community, creativity, diversity, excellence, integrity, and servant leadership. These values led XA to ask the question, "What could XA look like in the new century?" To accomplish this, 55 national, regional and district leaders, and CMIT directors met to affirm the values, vision, and mission, and outline seven strategies for the future. Leadership agreed the infrastructure and systems were in place in XA with missionary appointment well established, so XA could press ahead with new initiatives.

The Seven Strategic Initiatives for the 2000s
1. Implement strategic management
2. Increase quality staff training
3. Pioneer new groups
4. Equip students to be missional

5. Foster a culture of Spirit empowerment
6. Provide personnel support-raising training
7. Fund a national vision

These seven initiatives would create a framework for XA's development in the 21st century. Five of the seven initiatives got traction and concrete results were observed in the first decade by 2010. Staff training and assessment improved, coaching was initiated, new groups were pioneered, missions mobilization increased, the gifts of the Spirit/Spirit empowerment was evident in more groups and events, and widespread personal support training increased. By 2009, there were 19 support-raising trainers and support-raising training sessions available in all eight regions of the nation providing training to around 150 personnel each year. XA Missionaries, CAs, MAs, CMITs, and students and staff raising funds for mission trips and projects, and personnel from other departments and organizations attended the training venues.

Missions Mobilization Culture

The missions mobilization of XA students markedly advanced. A missions culture in XA gained considerable attention with XA student involvement in short-term missions trips; two-year mission associate assignments; becoming career missionaries overseas assigned to university ministry; and *Expeditions*, XA's missions magazine. *Expeditions* was distributed at all the regional SALTs and to each local XA group and awakened interests in missions. The magazine included missions stories from students who served overseas, field reports by AGWM regional directors, and listed opportunities worldwide for student involvement in missions.

The World Missions Summits

Five years after the XA World SALT, AGWM and XA established a strategic partnership that would host four World Missions

Summits (WMS) beginning in 2005, and held again in 2009, and two more in the next decade. The WMS exposes students to missions opportunities and challenges them to participate in a cross-cultural missions experience during their undergraduate years on campus. It was a clarion call to "every student goes, every student gives, and every student prays." Hundreds of students, graduates, and campus ministers each year went on missions assignments around the world. Other slogans emerged like, "give a year, pray about a lifetime," and "take the if and how out of missions and replace it with the when and where," that moved other students and staff to respond.

WMS included five aspects: 1) the large group gathering with students testimonies, missionary cameos, missions videos, prayer, powerful worship, challenging messages to go, give and pray, and opportunity to respond to a call to missions; 2) Prayer for the Nations, with colorful country flags, cultural indigenous clothing, and missionaries presenting challenges and opportunities where they serve; 3) Windows to the Word, where students experienced the smells, sights, textures, and sounds of each world region and learned about missions globally through interactive missional encounters; 4) Meals with a Missionary involved missionaries joining students for a meal and talking about their mission experience, life, and the countries where they served; 5) Exhibit Centers with artifacts, photos, and information and missionaries present to answer questions about the mission field.

The first two WMSs in 2005 and 2008 attracted more than 7,000 students, staff, and missionaries, with 1,500 responding to "give a year to missions, and pray about a lifetime of missions."

XA Females

Female student enrollment has outnumbered men on campuses since the late 1970s. Today nearly 60% of enrollment in universities and colleges is female, compared to 40% men. XA recognizes the need for more female campus ministers to minister to the large numbers of female college students. Beginning in the 2000s, more women in XA, especially wives, have earned ministerial credentials, and an increasing number of single and married females are ordained each year.

Reach the University Institute and CMIT

The Reach the University Institute (RUI) name replaced Institute of Campus Ministry (ICM) in 2000. Training campus ministry staff remains central to the national ministry center and continues each year and is conducted annually in Springfield, Missouri. During the decade, an average of 70 prospective campus leaders participated in RUI.

The RUI training is combined with the CMIT program, held on campuses nationwide. CMITs are typically nine to 10 months long (some extend from one year to two years). During the 2000s, two models of internship training were offered, the Classic CMIT and Hub CMIT model. The Classic model training is done on one campus under the leadership of the local campus director and team. The Hub model operates on multiple satellite campuses offering joint training out of one primary campus, but utilizing all staff from each of the satellite campuses, and periodically rotating to conduct training at one of the satellite campuses.

Pioneering Campus Ministry

Pioneering campus ministry experienced the greatest push with separate training first offered at RUI as early as 2005, and on local campuses or in a district that was starting new works. This was followed by pioneering boot camps along with assessment and coaching.

Student Institute of Campus Ministry

The Student Institute of Campus Ministry (SICM), a venue to train student leaders, started in 1993 in Washington state, and continues today. The first was called the NW SICM and it is held annually, involving several hundred students during the 2000s. Four more regional SICMs were launched in the 2000s: NE 1999, Central US 2001, Great Lakes 2002, and Atlantic Coast 2019, and another SE 2019 would be added in the next decade.

Exponential 2010s

4,599 colleges and universities
21,019,438 college students
723,277 international students enrolled in U.S. campuses
From 274 to 297 chartered Chi Alpha Groups
U.S. population: 308,745,538

What happened in the 2010s?

Barack Obama was president 2009-2017. Affordable health care. A 9.0 magnitude earthquake strikes Japan on March 11, 2011. "Occupy Wall Street" protesters condemned income inequality and the influence of money in politics. Arab Spring uprisings against authoritarian regimes in the Middle East: Tunisia, Egypt, Libya, Morocco, Yemen, and Bahrain. George Floyd and Black Lives Matter. British Petroleum's "Deepwater Horizon" offshore oil platform explodes April 10, 2010, killing 11 workers and dumping nearly five million barrels of oil into the Gulf of Mexico. Increasing number of attacks driven by racist, xenophobic, homophobic, anti-Muslim and/or anti-Semitic views. Osama bin Laden killed by U.S. special forces. "Me too" Movement. Same-sex marriage. Pope Francis elected. Marijuana legalized in Colorado. Solders began returning home from war in Afghanistan. Mass shootings at schools, theaters, grocery stores, malls, a music festival, parade, dance clubs, and various workplaces. A bitterly divided political campaign in 2016 ended with Donald Trump elected the 45th president. He served from 2017 to 2021.

CHAPTER 8

Exponential 2010s

Six Emphases in the 2010s

In 2010, XA sharpened the focus with six new emphases: Brand, Diversity, Resources, Systems, Transitions, and Network. Most of the progress in the decade was made with the first three emphases, along with a comprehensive study on XA's preferred future under the auspices of Systems.

Brand increased name recognition and identity. A new logo and promotional campaign is now utilized, along with a major redesign of the XA webpage. Local campus ministry webpages and marketing the XA ministry in using social media like Facebook, Twitter, TikTok, and Instagram enhanced communications locally and nationwide.

Diversity was initially adopted in 2005 calling for reconciliation of students to Jesus across all demographics. The XA Great Lakes region conducted the first African American Leadership Conference in 2011, recruiting and training diverse staff, adding diversity resources, and planting XA at HBCUs. Eight different HBCUs have organized local XA groups or a level of activity and outreach is underway on each campus. A minority mobilization fund was established to assist minority campus ministers, so by 2019, one third of the CMIT interns were minorities. In 2017-18, student diversity in XA represented 41% and staff diversity represented 19%. The 19% ethnic diversity accounted for 225 workers of the 1,200 affiliated personnel in XA. Resources and work groups were developed by the diversity task group to mobilize and equip minorities.

Resources for XA mostly came from local leaders and groups who posted on their website and used XA Facebook and Instagram to share ideas, resources, and events. By 2017, a plethora of digital resources: cross-cultural missions resources, small group leadership podcast, evangelism, and recordings from XA events like RUI and CMC, and links to other resources from other organizations were featured on the XA webpage. Many of the resources are organized around the four practices for healthy leaders introduced in 2013 (see below).

Systems got considerable attention in the 2010s. This was a major emphasis. Leadership had decided it was time for an organizational systems assessment to continue to prepare XA for the future. National XA had done comprehensive reviews of XA in 1977 and 1993. In 2009, a 17-member team met and selected a smaller task group to address the question, "What is a preferred future for XA?"

Other national campus ministry organizations were reviewed and studied, and Reformed University Fellowship (RUF) in the Presbyterian Church of America had the most similarities to XA, including a denominational model; credentialed ministers leading campus ministry; a strong evangelism arm of the church and major pipeline for ministers, missionaries, and congregants; active in church planting; and under the umbrella of the Mission to North America (MNA). XA operated in an almost identical way and under the auspices of AG U.S. Missions.

Ten years earlier (2000), the Presbyterian denomination restructured to have university ministry independent of MNA, and resulted in growth in groups and income that was staggering. XA saw great value in operating more like RUF, with greater autonomy from AG U.S. Missions, but remained linked to the AG General Council. A proposal was submitted for such a restructuring, but did not receive approval. XA would continue to operate as it had within the AG U.S. Missions structure as a department. Growth in XA has not stopped. Consideration for greater autonomy may be relevant in the future, so XA has complete oversight of its mission, missionaries, and money.

Transitions of Christian high school graduates going off to college was explored due to an ongoing concern that the church loses so many students after they graduate and go off to college. Studies show between 50% and 80% walk away from their faith after attending college. While parents and youth workers have much responsibility, XA played a crucial role in representing XA at church and youth services, and youth camps and conventions, to meet high schoolers bound for college to strengthen their faith as they transition to college.

Networking from college graduation to the marketplace and the church was another important emphasis during the 2010s. If transitions were about smoothly entering the front door of the university after graduating from high school, then networking was exiting the door of the university once a person graduates. The idea is to train and resource college graduates for post-university leadership roles and mobilize Spirit-filled marketplace "missionaries" and church-planting teams. This was an ambitious plan, but without adequate oversight and coordination networking did not reach its intended goals. In 2023, a new initiative for training alumni and marketplace Christians was launched.

What Makes Healthy XA?

With his final year of service, Dennis Gaylor conducted two events to bring together new and younger XA leaders in two forums in the fall of 2012 and another separate smaller gathering of experienced campus ministers in January 2013. With younger leaders representing every region of the nation, the forum was primarily a listening venue to get their pulse on XA at the local level and input into the national program and its future. The young leaders identified and affirmed XA strengths as Pentecostal, experiential, diverse, collegial, relational, missional, focused on making disciples, and a strong XA culture and identity. They also gave their input on how national XA can improve, and assist and resource them.

The second meeting engaged six experienced campus missionaries representing accomplished campus ministers leaders to address the question, "What makes healthy XA campus ministries?" They identified four components for healthy XA. The common elements in campus groups nationwide that represented local XA groups that were effective and healthy year after year in student involvement, making disciples, cross-cultural missions engagement, strong Spirit-led worship, and teaching and training are:

1. Healthy leaders
2. Disciple-making groups
3. Cross-cultural missions
4. Spiritual empowerment

When these four practices exist in XA, the result is spiritual maturity that ensures campus ministry health and longevity. The results of the 2012 forums and the 2013 healthy XA discussion and decisions, and follow up has major influence on XA's future as XA advances toward 2020 and beyond. Healthy XA influenced the appointment and agenda for the newly created Guiding Coalition, national staffing, themes and speakers for CMC, and resources like *XA Connections, Expeditions*, and the XA website.

A Farewell

Dennis Gaylor gave his final message, "Dreaming Together Our Biggest and Deepest Dreams," at the Imagine Conference, following the WMS III in Fort Worth Dec. 31, 2012. He outlined a vision for the future with 10 dreams, including establishing XA on Historically Black Colleges and Universities (HBCUs), resource churches to reach students at community colleges, increased participation in student cross-cultural missions, welcome and befriend 1% of the international students studying in the U.S., and plant university churches.

Gaylor retired in spring 2013, completing 35 years of service and four years as the district XA director for South Texas. When he retired, XA had been in existence for 60 years, 1953 to 2013. When he first became national director, he looked long term with the desire for XA to develop so young men and women, singles and couples, and families called to campus ministry would be able to fulfill a vocational dream in a XA career. This has been fully realized in the 21st century.

XA began national appointment for missionaries in 1992 with 12 personnel and by 2020 there were 323. Gaylor's orchestration of the historic and strategic move of XA from the National Youth Department/Church Ministries to AG U.S. Missions in 1986/87 resulted in hundreds of men and women having careers as campus missionaries.

Seventh National Director Appointed

The process took a year, and on March 25, 2014, the AG Executive Presbytery ratified E. Scott Martin upon the recommendation of the search committee and the executive director of AG U.S. Missions as the seventh national director of XA. With XA's vast nationwide development and the increased responsibility that the assignment entailed, Martin's position was upgraded to senior national director. Prior to assuming national leadership of XA, Martin had served as the student missions director in the national XA ministry for 18 years, and before this as the Arizona District XA director and campus minister at the University of Arizona in Tucson.

Martin is a visionary, prophetic, eternally optimistic, and a persuasive communicator. He single-handedly developed XA's student missions movement and partnership with AGWM that led to four World Missions Summits and thousands of students involved in missions. Martin also challenged his national resident staff team and all campus leaders with four principles: honor, respect, unity, and prayer. He has developed the largest residential national staff team and has seen the affiliated XA personnel grow exponentially, doubling since he became national director.

Guiding Coalition

He formed a guiding coalition with the area directors, national staff, and campus ministers that represented new and younger leaders from different geographical areas. The coalition was created to broaden the voice of influence into national XA initiatives and programs.

National Ministry Center

Martin articulated the purpose of the XA National Ministry Center to provide XA with apostolic covering, prophetic voices, keepers of the trust, administration, and bureaucracy. The national staff team is there to serve and resource XA leadership. One decisive action Martin took after assuming office was to have key national staff personnel locate in Springfield and to operate out of the national ministry center. Requiring national level staff members to be resident in Springfield strengthened and unified the national team, enhancing collaboration and implementation of vision and ministry.

National Executive Ministry Team

He established a seven-member national executive ministry team (EMT) to give administrative and spiritual leadership and oversight to all of XA. Qualified missionaries with full budgets assumed several national assignments. Martin redefined some roles nationally adding a program director, a field rep, training director, and expeditions director.

Office Expansion

By 2015, as more staff were added, the need for additional office space required adding a separate location in an AG satellite building. In 2019, policies no longer allowed missionaries and MAs (non-employees) to remain in the AG satellite office, so in 2020, national XA leased an office suite one mile from headquarters that accommodates XA missionaries and MAs.

Traveling Ministry

Martin travels extensively to meet with local XA campus leaders and speak to campus groups. He is invited to speak at district councils and churches, missions conventions, and represent XA at AG events, and to organizations outside of the AG. He also travels abroad with missions teams and to speak at world missions gathering. For the past few years, Martin has produced a national director's video blog each week, informing, challenging, and inspiring XA leadership nationwide.

When Martin and his wife, Crystal, first came to Springfield, Crystal became a public schoolteacher. She resigned her teaching position and joined her husband as co-student missions director so they could serve together. She earned her ministerial credentials in 2012 and completed a graduate degree in 2016. Their example of working together as a married couple encourages the missionary couples joining the national team and working in the ministry center to serve as couples, both with responsibilities. Since so many XA leaders and their partners serve together on campus, and an increasing number of couples both have ministerial credentials. The Martins are a great model of leadership.

Crystal Martin became the XAi director in 2010, and in 2017, she took a broader assignment as director of Cross-Cultural Missions, overseeing XA Internationals, Expeditions, Diversity, feedOne, and the global student movement, including the World Missions Summits.

Two Initiatives Launched in 2000
Come to Fruition in 2015

Strategic Management Models

The first initiative addressed procedures to steward the XA ministry in healthy XA components and in annual chartering, census taking and reporting, and ministry assessment. Mutual cooperation and accountability between national XA and district and local XA vis-á-vis enhanced and strengthened XA nationally and globally. There was genuine solidarity and unity and respect for one another.

Funding National Vision

XA began to make great strides in financial advancement. In 2017, a national XA Foundation was set up, and subsequently an Endowment Fund. Development of a national XA Alumni Association and an alumni digital newsletter sowed seeds into this vision. In 2019, national XA conducted its first XA Marketplace Summit in Washington, D.C.

Two More World Missions Summits Conducted in the 2010s

A third and fourth WMS occurred in 2012 in Fort Worth and in 2016 in Houston. Attendance at the third WMS was 4,225 and the fourth was 6,064. The combined response to the missionary call of these two WMS was just short of 3,000. These summits harnessed collegians who abandoned themselves to the lordship of Christ to "go, give, and pray."

At the third WMS in 2012, XA announced and launched its partnership with feedONE, a subsidiary of Convoy of Hope, a relief organization focused on feeding children and alleviating world hunger. It is considered XA's compassion arm. FeedOne provides meals to 500,000 children in 26 countries. University students have been challenged to participate in feedONE. A $10 gift feeds a child for an entire month. Local XA groups and individual students and regional SALTs have participated wholeheartedly and give generously. Each year during November, feedOne is emphasized to all of XA. Tens of thousands of dollars have been donated by XA students.

XA International Student Ministry (XAi)

Unprecedented opportunity exists today to reach international students from most nations studying on U.S. campuses. In 2015, international student enrollment in the U.S. reached more than one million. The world is at our doorstep. The large number of international students coming to receive Western education, away from family and their home culture, are open to considering the claims of Christianity like no other time before. There have been five national leaders serving XA's international student ministry since the 1980s. In 2010, a new name and logo, XAi, translating to

"XA Internationals" was introduced, and "every student welcomes" was added to the missions slogan; "every student goes, gives, prays, and *welcomes.*"

In 2016. the first international was appointed as the director of XAi ministry. Several XA missionaries received appointment to work primarily with international student ministry. The annual All Nations Conference for international students begun in 1993 celebrated its 25th anniversary in 2018. It continues meeting during the Memorial Day weekend annually. Regional Discover the Nations conferences for internationals begun in Texas now exist in most regions of the country. Training seminars and workshop for international student ministry regular occur at SALT, RUI, and CMC.

XA Student Centers

For years, states in the South Central/Midwest regions had XA houses and a few student centers. They are used for XA staff and intern offices, housing, Bible studies, leadership classrooms, outreach programs, study, fellowship meals, and smaller XA meetings. Their popularity increased in the 21st century. Additional XA houses have been secured in New Mexico, South Carolina, Wyoming, Georgia, and Pennsylvania.

In recent years, as XA has matured as an organization and is stronger financially, more groups have purchased, refurbished, and built new structures. Some of the newest properties include a coffee café in Missouri, apartments in Ohio and Illinois, a large new 10,000-square-foot building in Arkansas, a real estate complex converted to a XA student center in Texas, three churches refurbished to become student centers, and five fraternity houses. The XA complexes provide student and staff housing and sites for leadership training, and give greater visibility of XA on campus.

More Men and Women Attracted to XA

The RUI continues as XA primary training event for new and prospective campus ministers, combined with the CMIT. The number of individual and couples seeking to be campus ministers has accelerated. By 2013, attendance at RUI exceeded 100 and did so the next five years. Attendance exceeded 200 in 2018. In 2019, 264 attended.

New Directors Training

In 2016-2017, New Directors Training was introduced that enhanced specialized training for pioneers, second career, church staff, and emerging leaders.

Student Awakening

In May 2016, Martin received a prophetic word: "We are about to witness the greatest student awakening in history." He added, "We believe XA will play a strategic role in leading and stewarding this historic awakening." Several of his peers from other national campus ministry organizations share this vision, believing God is moving by His Spirit on the university campuses. An unprecedented unity amongst national collegiate ministries and churches concerned with reaching the university is spreading.

Epic 2020s

4,298 colleges and universities
19,928,000 college students
710,000 international students enrolled in U.S. campuses
From 297 reduced to 289 chartered Chi Alpha groups
U.S. population: 331,449,281

What is happening in the 2020s?

The 2020s began as a tumultuous decade: The onset of a deadly pandemic (COVID-19) that resulted in schools, restaurants, and businesses closing, unemployment skyrocketing, and deaths of 1,129,573 in the U.S. from the disease by the end of April 2023. There were widespread protests over systemic racism. The decade began with a deeply contentious election. On Jan. 6, 2021, following the defeat of- then U.S. President Donald Trump in the 2020 presidential election, a mob attacked the U.S. Capitol in Washington, D.C., in what was considered an insurrection. Joe Biden was inaugurated as president on Jan. 20, 2021. Blue Origin and SpaceX launched spacecraft with civilians in 2021. Juneteenth became a federal holiday. Withdrawal of U.S. troops from Afghanistan in August 2021. Russia invaded Ukraine February 2022. "A uniquely American problem" 163 mass shootings since the start of 2023 (more than one per day). *Roe v. Wade* overturned by the U.S. Supreme Court June 2022. AI ChatGPT. In February 2023, one of the largest and deadliest earthquakes in Turkey and Syria in a century claimed 55,700 lives. Silicon Valley Banks collapsed in 2023.

CHAPTER 9

Epic 2020s

The 2020s

Epic is the best word to describe XA in the 2020s, especially with the plans of the seventh senior national director for XA, E. Scott Martin. He has served since 2014. National XA had come a long way in creating an anointed and highly efficient student missions organization at every level with well qualified missionary leaders that are Spirit-led and Spirit-empowered.

The National Ministry Center

XA personnel with national assignments continue to serve out of the two national ministry centers in Springfield. The AG National Leadership and Resource Center (formerly known as AG headquarters) houses the primary national XA offices for Martin and the Executive Ministry Team (EMT), and the other office which is one mile south of the headquarters (known informally and symbolically as the "Jordan," named after the Jordan Creek that runs under the building in downtown Springfield, and the biblical reference of crossing the Jordan River) houses missionaries and MAs with national assignments.

In 2023, there are 41 resident and field personnel serving nationally, including the seven members of the EMT, 18 national field specialists (seven of whom serve outside Springfield), and 16 support staff. The national staff team consists of nationally appointed missionaries, missionary associates, and employees. They serve and resource XA leadership nationwide. Many would say XA has crossed the Jordan spiritually and symbolically and is advancing like no time in its history. In addition to resident staff, there are eight area directors and 46 district leaders, and a 25-member guiding coalition. The coalition includes the EMT and the eight area directors and 12 rotating local campus ministers representing the nation.

Campus Missions Conference

The theme for the 2022 Campus Missions Conference was "Spirit-Empowerment," one of the four components of healthy XA. The gathering, held in Phoenix, had a record attendance of almost 2,000, including 500 youth and children, and 75 infants. CMC convenes every four years.

Awakening on Campus

Martin challenges XA to pray for a spiritual awakening on America's campuses, and believes for a powerful move of the Holy Spirit. He and a number of national campus ministry organizational leaders confirmed in 2016 that God was speaking to them about a spiritual awakening on campuses.

In 2018, the "Every Campus" campaign was launched. Every Campus is defined as "a collaborative initiative seeking God for revival by making gospel communities on every campus a possibility." The organization identified 4,189 campuses: 1,179 have multiple ministries, 1,281 have a single ministry present, and 1,729 have no known ministry presence. Christians are challenged to identify an unreached or traditionally underserved campus and conduct a prayer walk, and when possible begin a ministry.

XA Diversity Task Group

In response, the XA Diversity Task Group has prioritized and identified HBCUs to train and place minority campus missionaries at several of these schools. Missionaries leading XA at a major university have expanded ministry to nearby technology and community colleges, and other campus leaders have started ministry at smaller state colleges and liberal arts and private schools.

Collegiate Day of Prayer

In 2010, several of these national leaders renamed and revived the Concert of Prayer for Colleges established in 1815 to the Collegiate Day of Prayer. This unified prayer occurs on the last Thursday of February. The purpose is to have every college and university covered in prayer. Ten years into it, every campus in the United States is adopted and prayed for by thousands of volunteers from campus ministries, churches, parents, students, and others.

Missionary Personnel Serving XA

What XA has become in the 21st century is directly linked to our missions philosophy and appointment of qualified missionary personnel and comprehensive training. By 2023, AG U.S. Missions reported 364 nationally appointed XA missionaries and spouses.

This does not tell the whole story. An entry-level position begun in 1997, the campus missionary associate or MA, increased by leaps and bounds in 26 years from 12 MAs to 908 in 2023. And the newest personnel category, the XA career associate, CA, introduced in 2019-20 with 60, has increased to 267 in 2023. Another 328 affiliated leaders including district missionary appointed, church staff, and volunteers, and nine candidate missionaries and spouses brings the total of XA personnel to 1,876 in 2023. The number of XA personnel has more than doubled since 2014.

RUI and CMIT Continue to Attract Campus Workers

RUI 2020 was skipped due to the pandemic, but in 2021, 398 attended making up for the missed year. In 2022, attendance returned a more-normal 245. Further refining of the intensive RUI and comprehensive training and the CMIT internship program remains front and center. There are currently 42 classic CMIT programs and 33 Hub model CMIT programs. In 2021–2022, there were 225 interns who completed the campus ministry training. One third are minorities.

Missions Mobilizations

With a strong commitment and engagement in cross-cultural missions, XA's impact is global. XA has designed a special orientation and training for world missionaries to assist them in hosting XA student missions teams. Every year, hundreds of student mission teams and campus ministry staff travel abroad to serve for two weeks, a month, a summer, or one to two years. In 2023, 3,676 students and staff participated in 219 stateside and 188 overseas mission trips. Each year a number of these students who graduate from college become career world missionaries with AGWM to work with university ministry and other missions programs. AGWM reports that 40% of career missionaries are coming from Chi Alpha. Campus missions are growing across the globe. Many of the regions and countries abroad have world missionaries assigned to university ministry. These missionaries have developed student conferences and staff training events, plus internship programs. AG university missions is represented in 75 nations. The fifth World Missions Summit is scheduled for 2025 in St. Louis.

Capital Campaign

In 2022, a Capital Campaign got underway to engage major donors to contribute to the vision of XA to increase organizational capacity, accelerate growth and diversity, and invest in future projects.

Regular and major donors are funding XA's development.

Martin Writes and Publishes a Book

In 2022, E. Scott Martin wrote and published a book, *Kingdom Authority: Kingdom Authority Defined and It Components.* He defines Kingdom authority biblically, and draws from his own personal experience in writing the book.

"The Awakening is Here"

The XA vision is strong. It is a call to reconcile students to Christ, transform the university, the marketplace, and the world. In Martin's January 2023 national director's video blog, he exhorted XA "the awakening is here." He stated, "Never in 40 years have I seen this many people coming to Christ and the ease with which it's coming."

Martin reported that SALT directors informed him that the regional student conferences held during the 2022-2023 Christmas/New Year's break and Martin Luther King Jr. holiday were the best in decades. The combined attendance of the nine SALTs was 6,702. The power of the Spirit was evident in each gathering.

The South Central SALT in Texas celebrated its 50th anniversary (1972-2022) with its largest regional SALT attendance of 2,200. Fifty years ago, only 23 attended the first SC SALT. Students and staff at the recent SC SALT received almost $30,000 offering to assist in planting XA in Southern California. Martin believes, "Our SALTs are a harbinger of what is to come in the spring semester and quarter." Students and staff at the North and South Plains SALTs combined received $107,000 for feedOne, XA's compassion partnership with Convoy of Hope.

Martin's national campus ministry colleagues agreed they, too, were experiencing an unprecedented move of God at their events and on campuses this academic year. "There are great numbers of students coming to Christ, being baptized in the Holy Spirit, and committing to missions." Martin exhorted XA leadership and students "to be a conduit of the awakening."

Chi Alpha Celebrates 75 Years

Chi Alpha will celebrate its 75th anniversary in 2028. What God is doing on campuses today is indicative of what is to come in the next five years and the next decade. We envision the far-reaching influence of Spirit-empowered Christian college students who are committed to God, to one another, and their responsibility in the world. Change the campus, change the world.

PART II — CHI ALPHA

15 CAMPUS MINISTER STORIES

The remainder of the book, Part II, features personal stories of Chi Alpha ministers who came to Christ, many through Chi Alpha, and became leaders in campus ministry. Most of the articles have been published in *AG News* since 2022, so they represent current examples of the Chi Alpha story. *AG News* is the official news agency of the Assemblies of God. These contemporary stories demonstrate today's Chi Alpha and represent why Chi Alpha became a major national campus ministry movement in the 21st century.

STORY 1

James Madison University, Harrisburg, Virginia
Campus Minsters: Joshua and Katie Moran

Although he uttered a "sinner's prayer" as a Baptist youth because he feared going to hell over unconfessed transgressions, Joshua Moran rarely attended church. Parties where he got drunk and swore a lot turned out to be more frequent gathering places. But soon after he began attending college, his life turned around.

"Chi Alpha found me at the University of Virginia," Moran says of the Assemblies of God U.S. Missions outreach on mainstream campuses. "I felt the Holy Spirit in a way I did not have the vocabulary for at the time."

Moran's grandmother Wanda Sears bought him a leather-bound study Bible, he joined a Chi Alpha small group on the campus in Charlottesville, and he ceased imbibing and cursing.

No one in his family had ever been to college. The self-confident Moran had lofty goals. He wanted to become a lawyer, be elected senator, and then run the free world. His Chi Alpha involvement altered his goals to other means of persuasion. He switched his major to religious studies.

He graduated in 2007, and he responded to the Chi Alpha student missions challenge to "give a year and pray about a lifetime." The following year, Josh and Katie Summers became the first UVA Chi Alpha interns. Josh and Katie married in 2009.

"I had a degree in religion, but during the internship I grew in ways I could never have imagined," says Moran, 36. "It was one of the most formative years of my life in learning as I was repeatedly challenged to be a disciple-maker. I knew I wanted to do Chi Alpha forever."

The Morans joined the Chi Alpha staff at the University of Virginia and planned to stay a couple of years. But they changed their minds. They built their dream home, began raising four children, and planned to remain at the school in ministry the rest of their vocational days. While rising to assistant director at the UVA Chi Alpha, Josh also took over as Chi Alpha director of the Potomac Ministry Network six years ago, a role he maintains.

U.S. missionary Pete Bullette has directed Chi Alpha at the University of Virginia for 20 years, taking it from a core group of 15 students to 500, now meeting in 50 small groups.

"I saw Josh go from a young Christian who never read his Bible to a person whose mind and character became more Christ-like," says Bullette, 44. "He has matured in his walk with Christ and is a deep follower of Jesus in so many ways."

Bullette commends Moran for his strong people skills, preaching gifts, and administrative abilities. "He brings a certain joy and energy to any room," Bullette says. "Josh is a Kingdom gem."

Twelve years into their UVA ministry, the Morans sensed a calling to launch a Chi Alpha ministry at James Madison University in Harrisonburg, Virginia. So they sold their recently constructed dream home and moved into a century-old fixer-upper a block from the JMU campus, which has more than 22,000 students. Those at Harrisonburg First Assembly, including pastor Jeff Ferguson, had been praying about ministering to college students and the church has been supportive of the couple's efforts.

JMU is one of the more selective schools in the nation in terms of applicants. The university offers 115-degree programs, with nursing, education, speech pathology, and sports management among the most popular educational pursuits.

The Morans, who are both ordained AG ministers and U.S. missionaries, started the ministry on campus in 2019 and shared responsibilities. The COVID-19 pandemic hit that first school year, forcing the Morans to be creative in their outreach efforts. Gatherings had to be held outside, with participants wearing masks and staying 10 feet apart.

While their four children are in school, Katie will take over the lead campus role as Josh spends more time with Potomac Ministry Network duties. Others on the JMU ministry team include Hunter and Julia Johnson, Rachel Colón, and intern Faith Funkhouser.

Josh succeeded U.S. missionary Stefanie Chappell as Potomac Ministry Network Chi Alpha director. She has known him for 14 years.

"I've seen him thrive as a young leader who took on more responsibilities with excellence, integrity, conviction, and influence," says Chappell, who since 2016 has been the national Chi Alpha field director overseeing eight area directors. "He has serious leadership skills and is really smart, which may not be the first thing you notice because he is so relational and fun."

Josh anticipates a time of growth at James Madison University's Chi Alpha in 2021-22.

"This could be our first normal year," he says. "We will have unrestricted social events for the first time. But small groups will still be the heartbeat of who we are."

Katie grew up in the AG and always wanted to be a part of Chi Alpha. Josh says in their first two years at JMU she discipled the majority of the staff and led the bulk of the meetings. He says the Church shouldn't lag behind the business world when it comes to promoting women leaders.

"For years, the Assemblies of God has said we are pro-women in ministry, but that is not always the reality," Josh says. "The task is too great for half the population to remain on the sidelines. This is biblical; we need all hands on deck."

Bullette says Katie shares her husband's heart for ministry.

"They have a lot of solidarity in the mission," Bullette says. "Josh has been a champion for women in leadership."

Chappell, 53, expects Katie to thrive as a leader.

"Katie is an outstanding discipler and preacher," says Chappell, who has been with Chi Alpha for three decades. "What both Katie and Josh bring to the table is essential."

"Lifetime Leaders, Chi Alpha directors at James Madison University have come a long way," by John W. Kennedy, originally in *AG News,* July 22, 2021.

STORY 2

Virginia Tech University, Blacksburg, Virginia
Campus Minsters: Anthony and Michele Saladino

During his senior year at William Patterson University in Wayne, New Jersey, Anthony Saladino lived with his girlfriend and had no interest in following Jesus. But fearing his soccer teammates had become too dependent on drugs, the physical education major urged them to quit smoking, snorting, and shooting up. They laughed at him.

Saladino's emotional outlook only grew worse when he broke up with his girlfriend. He needed a change of scenery.

So, in a semester exchange program the school offered, Saladino in 2000 enrolled for a semester at the University of Montana. On campus, he met a Christian woman named Jenn Sterns who invited him to church.

"The presence of God scared me to death," Saladino remembers. Worshipping at the altar, with his face on the floor, Saladino cried out to God. Subsequently, Saladino says, the Lord broke his addictions to drinking alcohol and hooking up with women.

Saladino had another revelation when he attended a Chi Alpha meeting held at the church.

"I heard an internal voice saying, *The cool people you are looking for are right here*," Saladino recalls.

As a college student, Saladino planned to become a soccer coach. But Chi Alpha altered his career.

For the past 14 years, the 44-year-old Saladino and his wife, Michelle — a 2005 graduate of James Madison University in Harrisonburg, Virginia — have directed the Chi Alpha chapter at Virginia Tech University in Blacksburg. It has grown to be one of the largest Chi Alpha groups in the U.S., with more than 400 students involved in meetings and/or Bible studies. There are a dozen staff members.

The Saladinos arrived at the school two years after the worst mass shooting on a U.S. university campus. In 2007, student Seung-Hui Cho used semi-automatic pistols to murder 32 people. In 2009, the Saladinos found some students still traumatized by the event.

In part, that is why the couple laid prayer as a foundation of the ministry. Five times a week, prayer sessions are held from 6:30-8:30 a.m.

"Our strategy has always been to invest in prayer to come against spirits," says Michelle, 40. "We have a unique prayer culture of 10 hours of prayer meetings a week. Hundreds of students have attended."

Challenges remain, however. Virginia Tech is an academically driven research school known for its engineering program. COVID-19 restrictions enacted the past couple of years limiting in-person gatherings didn't help.

"Hunger for God is less than we've ever seen," says Michelle, a credentialed Assemblies of God minister. "The pandemic worsened it, as students gravitate to the familiar and comfortable, including addictions to cellphones and other technology. The message of culture now is self-care and narcissism."

"The desire to live a sacrificial life is not as strong as it used to be," says Anthony, a U.S. missionary.

Nevertheless, the Saladinos have accomplished much, helping to deliver students from addiction, depression, suicidal thoughts, and other demonic oppression. Such activity isn't the norm at a STEM (science, technology, engineering, and math) school such as Virginia Tech.

At the annual Chi Alpha Reach the University Institute in June in Springfield, Missouri, the couple led a session on how to baptize people in the Holy Spirit.

"We do not rely on our own power," Michelle says.

"Our dependence on the Holy Spirit and culture of prayer as missionaries and as a movement, will be the difference between a fruitful, lasting transformation in the souls of our students' lives," Anthony says.

Mario Solari, Southeast Region director for Chi Alpha, believes the Virginia Tech ministry is fruitful because the Saladinos rely so heavily on the Holy Spirit. Solari, 58, says Anthony humbles himself in obedience to the Holy Spirit, which empowers him in situations of evangelism, prayer for healing, and baptizing people in the Holy Spirit.

"Anthony's desire to be obedient overcomes any natural tendency he may have to second-guess or be apprehensive about leadership," says Solari, who first led a Chi Alpha chapter in 1993 at Florida State University. Solari notes that Virginia Tech students have been saved and healed just by passing by a Chi Alpha gathering.

"The Virginia Tech group is truly Spirit-filled," says Solari, who has been pastor the past 15 years of Mosaic Church in Tallahassee, Florida. "The supernatural occurs regularly, even among those who are not Christians.

Solari, a U.S. missionary, also commends Saladino for mentoring student leaders, several of whom are now leading ministries elsewhere.

"The Chi Alpha ministry at Virginia Tech is not built on Anthony's personality," Solari says. "He is discipling and empowering leaders, and letting them flourish in the capacity to which God has called them."

"Broken for Service. Anthony Saladino reached a crisis point, found God, and never looked back," by John W. Kennedy, originally appeared in *AG News*, Aug. 31, 2022.

STORY 3

Ohio State University, Columbus, Ohio
Campus Minsters: Kenji and Sierra Kuriyama

U.S. missionary Kenji Kuriyama has a bachelor's degree in classical music composition from Louisiana State University. He has a master's degree as well as a doctorate in classical music composition from Indiana University.

At the age of 9, Kenji Kuriyama first entertained the notion of someday becoming a music professor. He achieved his goal while a graduate student at Indiana University's prestigious Jacobs School of Music, as a music theory and ear training instructor to 120 students. He had seven assistants under him as lab instructors.

"I loved teaching so much," says Kuriyama, 35. "I felt I was born to do it."

The gig served as an important résumé builder, opening the door for Kuriyama to take his career in whatever direction he wanted. In addition to playing piano proficiently, he also knows how to play guitar, bass, percussion, violin, and trumpet. He composed his first classical music piece at 14.

More than academics occupied Kuriyama during his time at Indiana University. He helped restart the Chi Alpha chapter at the school with U.S. missionary Derek Britt.

"I saw salvations and baptisms right and left," says the affable Kuriyama. "I wanted to see more."

Despite his budding music career, Kuriyama decided to give a year to Chi Alpha as a missionary while finishing his doctoral dissertation. The experience changed his vocational trajectory.

"I realized I was more in love with ministry and missions than music," recalls Kuriyama. "What tipped the scales for me was which career could make the most impact for the Kingdom."

Kuriyama ended up staying on the Chi Alpha Indiana staff for nine years.

"He was the heart and soul of Indiana University Chi Alpha," says Britt, 39. "It says a lot about him that he joined us with his talents and giftings after earning a Ph.D. from the best music school in the country and becoming a professor."

Now Kuriyama is leading Chi Alpha Campus Ministries at Ohio State, a school with over 61,000 students on its main campus in Columbus, including 36.2% nonwhite collegians. The student body is comprised of more than 6,000 internationals from over 100 nations.

Kuriyama relaunched the chapter just after the COVID-19 pandemic hit. Fifty students participated in the 2021-22 school year and Kuriyama anticipates there will be 14 small group leaders ready when the fall semester kicks off. The chapter has five staffers, all of whom came from Indiana University.

U.S. missionary Jeff Alexander is familiar with both Kuriyama and Britt. Alexander spent nearly a decade as Chi Alpha district director in Indiana before joining the Chi Alpha national office in Springfield, Missouri, in 2017 as personnel director. Prior to serving in Indiana, Alexander led the Ohio State Chi Alpha chapter for 10 years. He believes Kuriyama's academic accomplishments garner respect and credibility among students as well as faculty.

"Kenji has a Ph.D. from a good music school that he could use in many places," says Alexander, 52. "But he feels the greatest investment he can make is in discipling students who go all over the world. Plus this shows God uses really smart people."

Kuriyama is the son of a Japanese father and a Costa Rican mother. His parents — Takeshi Kuriyama and Beatrice Granados — met at a supermarket in San José, Costa Rica's capital. His father operated a flower shop inside the store and his mother worked as a cashier. The cultures can be at odds.

"The Japanese part of me makes me want to be punctual," the humorous Kuriyama says. "The Latino part, not so much."

Kuriyama grew up a cultural Catholic, never attending church. As an international first-year student at Louisiana State University, he arrived on campus with no friends. Jacob Benda, a music classmate, invited him to a Chi Alpha meeting. Kuriyama got involved in the group, and a year and a half later in 2007 made a Christian commitment.

"Through friendships and connections, I found Jesus," recalls Kuriyama, who became the worship leader his senior year.

He continued his involvement in Chi Alpha while enrolled at Indiana University at Bloomington. Kuriyama attended Ellettsville First Assembly of God, a suburban church where he met future wife, Sierra, a rural Indiana native. The couple wed in 2016. They have a daughter and a son. Sierra, like Kenji, is a U.S. missionary. She preaches and leads Bible studies at Chi Alpha.

More than half the attendees are nonwhite, in part because of Kuriyama's presence leading the ministry at a campus with the third largest student body in the nation.

"It speaks volumes that Chi Alpha entrusted a nonwhite person to be director at a flagship university," says Kuriyama. "I'm biracial, bilingual, and bicultural. Like the apostle Paul, I can be all things to all people in order to win some to Christ."

Following the advice of Paul in citing 1 Corinthians 9, Kuriyama has learned to play the card game euchre to find community with one group of students and started lifting weights at 6 a.m. to connect with another.

In recent years, Chi Alpha has made recruiting more ethnically diverse staffers a priority.

"We believe in giving international students and ethnic minorities the opportunity to lead," Kuriyama says.

Alexander considers Kuriyama humble, Spirit-dependent, and a joyful encourager. That bodes well for relating to students, especially internationals.

"His Chi Alpha leadership breaks the stereotype of Christianity being an Americanized religion," Alexander says.

Kuriyama says his career change didn't bother his parents, who primarily had concerns about him providing for his family rather than what he did for a living. He says he has no regrets in choosing ministry over music.

"I thought teaching music would be the best job in the world for me, but I was wrong," Kuriyama says. "I have truly found the best job in Chi Alpha."

"Composing a New Theme, Former music professor Kenji Kuriyama leads Chi Alpha at The Ohio State University," by John W. Kennedy, originally appeared in *AG News*, July 26, 2022.

STORY 4

Indiana University, Bloomington
Campus Minsters: Derek and Jordan Britt

Derek Britt had landed his dream job, ministering to college students as a staff pastor at The Caring Place, a large Assemblies of God church in his native Indianapolis.

But eventually Britt sensed God calling him to minister to students on a secular college campus rather than inside church walls. Britt, 39, believes ministry to young adults needs to look different than a generation ago because U.S. culture has changed so much.

"Now 60% of Americans have no interest in church and 90% of college students are not involved in any ministry," says the fast-talking Britt. "How do we position ourselves for maximum impact?"

Britt, who had been raised in the Assemblies of God, knew the Fellowship had an effective ministry on secular campuses called Chi Alpha. He served a 10-month Chi Alpha internship at Florida State University before returning in 2011 to his beloved Indiana, where his entire family and the family of his wife, Jordan, reside. The Britts have two sons.

Britt saw an opportunity to minister on one of the largest campuses not only in the Hoosier State but the entire country: Indiana University (IU) in Bloomington, which has an enrollment of over 45,000 students.

But Britt had a problem. The Chi Alpha group on campus had ceased to function more than a decade earlier. He didn't quite need to start from scratch, however. Graduate student Kenji Kuriyama launched the group while Britt began itinerating as a U.S. missionary. Kuriyama now is a U.S. missionary serving as Chi Alpha director at The Ohio State University.

The attraction model of yesteryear — expecting students to come to Chi Alpha meetings because they, or their parents, attend church — no longer is enough, Britt says.

Instead, Britt and his staff have developed a missional incarnational small group discipleship model designed to allow Jesus to transform the lives of students and unleash their spiritual potential.

Consequently, Chi Alpha involvement at IU is not limited to the traditional safe church service settings.

"We need to go on their turf, to live in their world," Britt says. "We need to think differently. We need to know our neighbors." So, Chi Alpha staff or student leaders intentionally join the soccer team, become part of the campus bicyclist enthusiast club, and befriend international students. It also means not being afraid to engage leaders of fraternities or even LGBTQ activists.

"Students are deconstructing their faith as never before," Britt says. "The world has changed dramatically in the last decade."

The aftermath of COVID-19 restrictions is impacting the lives of college students even further, according to Britt. Many collegians, isolated in dormitories for entire semesters, have diminished social skills as a result, he says.

Although Indiana might be considered a conservative state, the IU campus definitely has a long tradition as "progressive." After all, this is the school where professor Alfred Kinsey started the Institute for Sex Research in 1947.

During the pandemic, Britt became a ride-hailing driver and found out just how far away from God some students are. Rather than concentrating on studies, Britt encountered students enmeshed in illicit drugs, alcohol binges, and stripper performances.

"How do we reach that group of people?" Britt wonders. "We need to find a neutral ground. But it's going to take multiple years of investment."

One such Chi Alpha team member who did so is Chris Anderson, who regularly pedaled on 50-mile bike rides with classmates while finishing his masters' in business administration degree. Anderson also participated in the Little 500, an annual track cycling race that attracts over 25,000 spectators.

Sports are a great entry point for relationships and discussions, according to Britt, who played soccer on a team that went to national competition when he attended the AG's Southeastern University in Lakeland, Florida. He still coaches high school soccer.

In preparation for Britt relaunching the IU Chi Alpha, U.S. missionary Jeff Alexander, then Chi Alpha director for the Indiana District, took him to visit other campuses with a thriving Chi Alpha ministry. Alexander says Britt gleaned the best of each. That included the missional heartbeat and lordship of Christ at Sam Houston State University under U.S. missionary Eli Gautreaux and the strength and multiplication of small groups at the University of Virginia under U.S. missionary Pete Bullette.

"Derek is a high-capacity learner," says Alexander, who now is Chi Alpha's national people and health director in Springfield, Missouri. "What sets Derek apart is he follows through on learning. Derek has the ability to lead a large team to be an effective army; a lot of people don't."

This fall the IU Chi Alpha will have three dozen staff members ministering to 425 students expected to attend small groups.

Alexander says Britt — who succeeded him as Chi Alpha director for the AG Indiana District—has captured the ministry's emphasis to think outside the box.

"We exist on campus to take the gospel to people who won't show up at our meetings," says Alexander, 52. "Derek is willing to take risks to engage people groups. He is tremendous at casting vision."

The Indiana University Chi Alpha team also is focusing this fall on a branch campus in Indianapolis that is a unique partnership between IU and Purdue University: IUPUI. Nine team members will be at the school once the semester starts.

"Thinking Differently on Campus, Indiana University Chi Alpha takes ministry to various subgroups," by John W. Kennedy, originally appeared in *AG News*, Aug. 22, 2022

STORY 5

University of Central Arkansas, Conway
Campus Minsters: Jennifer Schiefer and Matt Carpenter

When Jennifer Schiefer began her studies at the University of Central Arkansas (UCA) in 2001, she considered herself a firm agnostic, convinced that a person couldn't be both intelligent and a Christian.

"For me, believing in Jesus was like believing in Santa Claus," says Schiefer, 39. "It seemed to defy logic."

As with many of the nonreligious in church-saturated Arkansas, Schiefer certainly had contact with Christians. But her high school classmates failed to provide adequate answers to questions such as, *How did Noah fit all those animals on an ark?* Or, *Why does God allow pain?*

Often, her intellectual queries would illicit blank stares or glib remarks such as, *You've just got to have faith!* At the time, Schiefer had none.

The first week on campus in Conway, Schiefer went to a Chi Alpha gathering — on accident. She saw a flyer advertising an event with a band. She appreciated the music, but not so much the lyrics. Jesus kept popping up in the words of the choruses.

"It's not that I hated Christians," says the straightforward Schiefer. "I just thought they were stupid."

Still, Schiefer left the initial meeting with a nagging sensation that she had a void in her life. That first semester, several of her dormmates who treated her with respect regularly went to Chi Alpha gatherings and they invited her along. Soon she began attending every Monday night.

"I found friendship before faith," Schiefer says. "My classmates weren't intimidated by my lack of faith or my asking questions." In group sessions, students began discussing a book written by onetime atheist Lee Strobel, *The Case for Faith: A Former Journalist's Personal Investigation of the Evidence for Jesus.* Schiefer started grappling with tough spiritual questions.

One evening, U.S. missionary Matt L. Carpenter, director of Chi Alpha at UCA, preached a message on "What Keeps Us from God?"

"The topic terrified me." Schiefer remembers. "I had based my life on what I could predict, control, and understand."

Carpenter asked attendees to write out, anonymously, their hindrances to God. Schiefer scribbled, *I'm afraid.*

In his daily quiet time with God, Carpenter prayed persistently for the needs the students described, especially the one who confessed to fear.

Her second semester, Schiefer loyally went to Chi Alpha small group meetings as well as worship services, sensing a mysterious sense of God's presence through the presence of others.

"My skepticism began turning into a desperate longing for a God I didn't know," Schiefer says. During the summer before her sophomore year, Schiefer agreed to participate in a 10-week discipleship training—even though she hadn't made a commitment to Christ yet. Carpenter saw how God had begun changing the heart and mind of the honors student.

At the course, Schiefer says she heard the voice of God speak for the first time, intoning, *Jennifer, I love you.*

"I just sat on the floor and wept," Schiefer recalls. "There was no altar call, no reciting a 'sinner's prayer.' I just recognized I had fallen in love with Jesus."

By her sophomore year, Schiefer started leading Bible studies. She graduated with a graphic design degree from UCA, but by the end of her schooling, she understood God had laid a path for full-time ministry with Chi Alpha, the group where she had formed lifelong friendships and found an eternal purpose. She has been on staff at Chi Alpha at UCA since 2006, working under the tutelage of Carpenter, who has been director at the school for 22 years.

"My background gives me a point of compassion for the person who isn't certain yet, the legitimate resistance people have of not being able to surrender their heart," Schiefer says. "I remember how lonely it felt to struggle to believe and not being able to do so."

Schiefer encourages those who have a longtime faith not to dread engaging with those who don't.

"We should never fear honest questions, even if we don't know all the answers," says Schiefer, an ordained AG minister and U.S. missionary. "We can wrestle through it."

The UCA Chi Alpha chapter is one of the largest in the U.S., with 800 students showing up regularly for services and/or small groups. Schiefer sometimes encounters students who claim to be saved, yet don't really know the basics of Christian life.

"I want to help people come to a deep heart knowledge of God," Schiefer says.

The UCA Chi Alpha has 140 student leaders, 20 interns, and 15 staff members. Schiefer is intern administrator and oversees women's discipleship. She also is one of eight executive presbyters for the Assemblies of God Arkansas District.

Carpenter, 49 has watched Schiefer blossom into a passionate follower of Jesus. He has come to trust her implicitly.

"Jen gets revelation from God and has a strong mind," says Carpenter. "God has filled her with wisdom and she functions with a lot of pastoral leadership. Jen is deliberate and doesn't waste words."

Carpenter believes prayer is responsible for the growth of Chi Alpha on campus. In 2020, the ministry opened a $2.3 million facility on campus debt-free.

"No Longer Struggling to Believe, Jennifer Schiefer isn't afraid to engage non-Christian students in deep conversations. She's been on the other end" by John W. Kennedy, originally appeared in *AG News*, Sept. 13, 2022.

STORY 6

Xavier University of Louisiana, New Orleans
Campus Minsters: Morgan and Isaac Fulton

U.S. Missions career associate Morgan Fulton and her husband, Isaac, have entered their second year as Chi Alpha directors at the nation's only Catholic Historically Black College and University (HBCU) campus, Xavier University of Louisiana.

Xavier is known as a pipeline for graduating Black students going to medical school. It is rated third academically among 79 HBCUs in the latest *U.S. News* rankings. The school in New Orleans attracts students from 32 states, with females accounting for 77% of enrollees.

Before Xavier, both Morgan and Isaac spent several years on the Chi Alpha staff at Tulane University, where they initially served as interns. They married in 2018.

While on staff at Tulane, Isaac spent parts of six years building connections at Xavier. Xavier had no ministry like Chi Alpha before.

Thirty students attend weekly life group meetings and a monthly worship service. The Fultons figure few premed students taking full course loads can commit to two gatherings each week.

"They're coming in often as nominal Christians," says the soft-spoken and mannerly Isaac, 30. "They may have gone to church on Sunday growing up, but they don't abide with God the rest of the week. We want to teach them how to have a personal relationship with the Lord, how to share the gospel, and how to make disciples who make disciples."

"Those who grew up in cultural Christianity don't have a relationship that affects how they spend their money, what they watch on media, how they speak, and who their friends are," says Morgan, 31.

Morgan, who is an ordained Assemblies of God minister, attended Louisiana Tech, where she earned an early childhood education degree. Isaac is a graduate of the University of New Orleans, where he received a psychology degree. Both stayed active in Chi Alpha during their college years.

After she finished her bachelor's degree, Morgan didn't have peace about teaching. Isaac applied to graduate programs en route to a psychology career, but sensed God telling him he could help people in a different and better way through Chi Alpha.

Morgan now is part of the Chi Alpha Diversity Task Force, which has a goal of doubling the number of HBCU campuses — currently 10 — on which the AG ministry is active.

"The Assemblies of God is one of the most diverse Christian movements," says Morgan, who spent a couple of years leading Chi Alpha women's ministries at Loyola University. "One of my callings is seeing other women who look like me walking into leadership."

Isaac in turn is committed to ethnic diversity.

"I want to see students and staff of all races feel welcome at all levels," Isaac says.

U.S. missionary Matthew DeGier, citywide team leader for Chi Alpha in New Orleans, over the years has provided pastoral and organizational support for the Fultons, who have no staff help at Xavier University.

DeGier, 42, believes the Fultons, have excelled at Xavier.

"Isaac's fruitfulness is striking and the group has flourished," DeGier says. "As full-time missionaries embedded in the community, they have an opportunity to encourage students in a way part-time volunteers or even church staff can't."

DeGier, who planted the Chi Alpha chapter at Tulane in 2003 with his U.S. missionary wife Jen, lauds Isaac for his consistency and listening abilities. He commends Morgan for her unflagging optimism and hospitality.

"Chi Alpha is starting to pay attention to HBCUs," DeGier says. "There is a great need and opportunity to disciple this generation of Black leaders in America."

Despite its location in the South, Tulane is a highly secularized school and often voted among the nation's top "party schools" in surveys, according to DeGier. But he is grateful for opportunities to evangelize and disciple students from foreign lands.

"We get to represent Jesus to folks from all over the world," DeGier says. "Some of them stay in the U.S., but many go home, sometimes to places where there is little representation of Jesus."

"Finding Favor at Xavier, Students at the nation's only Catholic HBCU respond to Chi Alpha's Morgan and Isaac Fulton," by John W. Kennedy, originally appeared in *AG News,* Sept. 19, 2022.

STORY 7

University of Vermont, Burlington, Vermont
Campus Minsters: Joe and Rachel Gavin

While enrolled at the prestigious New England Conservatory of Music (NEC) in Boston, the studious Joe Gavin practiced eight to 10 hours daily playing his clarinet.

The ambitious New York native had a clear goal at the oldest independent music conservatory in the nation: land a job on a metropolitan orchestra. However, the longer he stayed at the school, the more disillusioned Gavin became. His professors seemed unhappy and unfulfilled. He realized a music career might not be such a terrific aspiration after all.

During his sophomore year, Gavin connected with a small group of undergraduates on campus at a student-run organization called Chi Alpha. Despite his arduous rehearsal schedule, he made time to attend meetings.

"I saw in those students something I had never seen before: a real vibrant faith, a love of God," recalls Gavin, 44. "Some of them were incredible musicians, but they weren't controlled by music like I was. I'd get depressed if I hadn't performed to perfection."

Gavin, raised in a home with good values and a belief in God — yet little spiritual depth — decided he wanted what his classmates in Chi Alpha possessed. Yet it took him more than a year of wrestling with God to fully commit.

"The story of the rich young ruler haunted me," Gavin remembers. "For a while, I wasn't really willing to give up everything and follow Jesus."

A friend named Chris Dollard intentionally kept nudging Gavin. Finally, during his junior year at a Chi Alpha retreat, Gavin was baptized. Upon graduation from NEC in 2000, Gavin rejected several music-related job offers and decided to forgo pursuing graduate school. Instead, he traveled across the country to Western Washington University (WWU) in Bellingham to become an intern in Chi Alpha's Campus Missionary-in-Training program. At WWU, he met his future wife, Rachel Spradley, who served as a Chi Alpha staff member. Rachel got involved with Chi Alpha as a student at the University of Louisiana-Lafayette.

Gavin's parents expressed concern upon learning of their son's career choice. They had invested a great deal of money in allowing their youngest of four children to pursue musical training. His mom, Leona, even cried. However, eventually his parents came to support his campus ministry work.

After a 2-year internship and an additional four years on staff at WWU, Gavin headed back to New England in 2008 with Rachel to pioneer Chi Alpha Christian Fellowship at the University of Vermont. The school in Burlington, as well as the state overall, have a secular reputation. The University of Vermont, founded in 1791, became the first such institution to open in the U.S. with no religious affiliation.

"I wanted to go to a place of spiritual need," says Gavin, a U.S. missionary. The University of Vermont isn't known for the spirituality of its first-year students. A survey of the incoming 2025 class revealed only 3% identified as "exclusively Christian."

The school is more noted for its environmental studies program, social justice initiatives classes, and LGBTQ support groups. Gavin has significant hurdles to overcome in reaching the 13,292 who are enrolled.

"Not many of the students have church experiences," says Gavin, an ordained Assemblies of God minister. "There is no felt need for Christian community. Many are likely to be angry and distrustful toward evangelicals."

Still, the kindly, soft-spoken Gavin eyes opportunities.

"Students in this generation seem isolated and alone, despite being so connected through social media and other avenues," Gavin says. "Many are longing for meaningful relationships."

As happened with Gavin earlier, Chi Alpha stalwarts on campus tend to join the group at the invitation of a friend who expresses genuine concern.

"A student may attend for months without being a Christian," Gavin says. "They feel they belong before they believe. They will experience a prolonged courtship with Jesus."

Assisted by staff pastors Daniela and Isaac Shoulderblade as well as U.S. missionary associate Lisa Marie Thibault (who serves with Intercultural Ministries), the Chi Alpha chapter sponsors a weekly meal for 50 students.

"It's a lot of time, energy, and resources, but it's worthwhile," Gavin says. "More are coming, especially international students, who may experience the presence of God for the first time."

Gavin serves as the Chi Alpha district director for the Northern New England Ministry Network. Rachel, who initially served as director of the University of Vermont Chi Alpha, now is a paraeducator at Porters Point Elementary School in Colchester, Vermont. The Gavins, married 16 years, also stay busy with their three children.

These days, Gavin's clarinet mostly stays in the closet, although he once in a while — when ministry efforts seem unproductive and discouraging — wonders what might have been. Such moments also occur when he hears about a former classmate who now is conducting a major symphony or touring as a performing artist.

But then he remembers the everlasting rewards of following Jesus.

"I've been given a life of meaning and purpose," Gavin says. "God allows me to share life and the journey of faith with some incredible young men and women from all over the world, and I have the privilege of seeing them transformed by His grace and love."

Mike Olejarz mentored Gavin both as a student and when he launched the Vermont Chi Alpha. Olejarz, who spent 15 years overseeing Chi Alpha chapters in Southern New England, thinks Gavin is the perfect fit in the Green Mountain State.

"The Lord is using Joe in the secular school setting," says the 63-year-old Olejarz, who is a Chi Alpha national training team specialist based in Charlottesville, Virginia. "His low-key, easy-going nature helps. He's a good listener and he's not threatened by challenges."

Olejarz, who is in his 40th year with Chi Alpha, says Gavin has built a healthy group at Vermont through service projects, missions trips, and friendship evangelism.

"Joe has persevered on a tough New England campus," Olejarz says. "He keeps plugging away with kindness. He's got grit."

Sam Chevalier, a postdoctoral researcher in the field of power and energy at the Technical University of Denmark in Copenhagen, says Gavin impacted his decision to stay in academia. Chevalier engineers optimization and control algorithms which enhance the efficiency, security, and stability of future power grids.

"Joe helped me think deeply about the importance of Christians doing work which will have impact across all facets of society and the marketplace," says Chevalier, 29. "During the summer I was transitioning into graduate school, Joe's teachings really helped me find peace and clarity in my decisions."

Chevalier says Gavin taught him that all work, even if not explicitly "Christian" in nature, can be sacred.

"I clearly remember Joe fostering conversations in Chi Alpha about how we as Christians need to embrace the here-and-now problems of this world, just as Jesus did," Chevalier says. "Joe thought and taught deeply about the questions and problems that students at our school were asking."

Chevalier says Gavin mentored him about the importance of discipleship, which he will utilize next year when he joins the department of Electrical and Biomedical Engineering at the University of Vermont as a professor running his own lab. He says Gavin led him to understand his Christian faith in a deeper way via well-read, scholarly, and properly contextualized information, followed by honest and personal reflection.

"While I don't have all of the answers, I often use the tools Joe implicitly taught me when I am considering challenging spiritual questions," Chevalier says. "Without a doubt, my uncompromised faith is both stronger and better equipped to engage with modern cultural issue because of Joe Gavin."

"Performing to a Different Tune. Once hopeful of playing in a professional orchestra, Joe Gavin finds contentment in leading Chi Alpha at the University of Vermont," by John W. Kennedy, originally appeared in *AG News*, Oct. 31, 2022.

STORY 8

University of Hawaii at Mānoa
Campus Ministers: Jeremy and Debora Anderson

At the age of 17, Jeremy Anderson had affiliation with a Bay Area gang and plotted to kill a young man who had raped his ex-girlfriend. On the evening he planned to carry out the deed, Anderson instead acquiesced to a dinner invitation from his praying grandparents. He reluctantly went along with his elder relatives to ARCO Arena to hear a speaker they vaguely described as famous. That night in 1995, at the invitation of evangelist Billy Graham, Anderson accepted Jesus as his Savior.

"I had never tried Jesus, I never understood the gospel," says the trim and buff Anderson. "I got saved in more than one way. I would have ended up in prison or dead if I didn't go to the revival, because I would have killed that guy."

Instead, Anderson graduated from California State University-Stanislaus in 2004, then went on to become Chi Alpha Campus Ministries director at the school in Turlock after serving on staff for four years. Subsequently, he oversaw planting Chi Alpha outreaches on five other campuses in three counties that comprise the Central Valley Chi Alpha along the Highway 99 corridor: Modesto Junior College, the University of California Merced, Merced College, Fresno State, and Fresno City College.

Anderson met his bubbly wife of 19 years, Debora (who is of Portuguese descent), during his intern year in Turlock. In 2019, the couple — along with their four children — moved to Santa Cruz to start another Chi Alpha chapter with a team of missionaries at the University of California branch there.

An unusual feature of all these Chi Alpha chapters is a "free spiritual readings" booth, where team members explain Scriptures and offer prayers with non-Christians. Students experiencing trials and heartaches stop by, as well as those who are simply curious.

The outreaches are dependent on the gifts of the Holy Spirit. Staff and students pray extensively about their encounters beforehand, and often receive words of wisdom or knowledge for those who stop.

Students who visit a booth or tent sometimes are healed physically, or have a dream interpreted. Before a student departs, he or she is always asked if there is any reason why a commitment to follow Jesus shouldn't be made immediately.

"When they come to Christ through spiritual gifts, they become operational in those gifts," says Anderson, an ordained Assemblies of God minister. "We trust in the Holy Spirit's anointing more than our ability to persuade."

At Turlock, openness about past mistakes is a hallmark of both the large meetings and small group gatherings. Being part of the group requires a hefty dose of authenticity, as well as vulnerability. Framed images and mini biographies of students adorn one wall of the meeting room, summarizing the stark realities of past struggles with drunkenness, sexual promiscuity, drug dealing, homelessness, pornography addiction, and abortion. Testimonies wrap up with how the students found hope in Jesus.

Remarkably, the same framed testimonies are displayed in various other spots around campus — not to shock, but to evangelize. They are open invitations to those searching for genuineness to become part of the group. Likewise, at certain venues on campus, Chi Alpha students speak at open-air outreaches nicknamed "I am your sign."

In these amplified testimonies, students reveal their deep, dark secrets — life as it used to be — before culminating with how they found freedom in Christ.

Since 2015, the Andersons have served as Chi Alpha West Coast area directors, overseeing operations in California, Nevada, Arizona, and Hawaii.

In September, the Andersons moved to Hawaii to supervise a young adult team of six led by Filipino-American Jeffrey Chalko-Mique and his wife, Kelsey, who are relaunching the Chi Alpha chapter at the University of Hawaii at Mānoa. Other couples involved are Roneel and Andrea Chaudhary (Indian/Fijian and Hispanic) and Surr and Hailey Vang (Hmong and Indonesian/Euro-American).

The ethnic cultural mix is perfect for the campus, Anderson maintains.

"We have a conviction that diversity on earth should be like it is in heaven — every tribe, tongue, and nation," Anderson says. "Hawaii is a strategic place for many reasons. Students from all 50 states are on the University of Hawaii campus, and one-third of students on the islands are internationals."

Few students possess an evangelical Christian background, however. And despite the idyllic setting, University of Hawaii students ranked the third "least happy" in a recent Princeton Review academic study.

"We want to help them find true happiness in following Christ," Anderson says.

Anderson expects to duplicate the techniques that have been effective in California, such as "spiritual readings," in Hawaii.

"Some call it encounter evangelism." Anderson says. "People who go into a tent to receive a free spiritual reading are open to receive the Holy Spirit."

Jeffrey and Kelsey Chalko-Mique welcome the Andersons' leadership.

"Jeremy and Debora have spent five years building relationships in the Hawaii District" says the 31-year-old Jeffery, who serves on the Chi Alpha Diversity Task Force. "They have made it easier for the rest of the team."

"They are experienced in mentoring pioneering directors and staff teams," says Kelsey, 26.

When Anderson took over as director at CSU-Stanislas, no minority students attended Chi Alpha meetings. Whites quickly became the minority as Anderson befriended students coming from such diverse nations as Saudi Arabia, Japan, and India because of the comparatively low educational costs.

"Early on we were very intentional about genuinely embracing students from other nations," Anderson says. "We don't want to be shocked when we get to heaven."

"Aloha Relaunching, Chi Alpha starts again at the University of Hawaii," by John W Kennedy, originally appeared in *AG News*, Oct. 24, 2022

STORY 9

University of Tennessee-Knoxville
Campus Ministers: Tyler and Brooke Martin

Born and raised in Arkansas, Tyler and Brooke Martin never figured they would move away from the Natural State. Both grew up in Christian families, with Tyler's father Kenny Martin serving as a pastor and Brooke's dad Billy Warren as a longtime deacon.

Although Brooke left Arkansas briefly to attend Central Bible College and Evangel University in Springfield, Missouri, Tyler went to the University of the Ozarks in Clarksville, Arkansas. Upon marrying in 2015, they already had decided on careers as U.S. missionaries serving with Chi Alpha.

They both served internships at the University of Central Arkansas in Conway, which has one of the most robust Chi Alpha chapters in the U.S., and they spent another year as missionary associates at Arkansas State University

The Martins asked the Lord for direction in leading them to be directors of a Chi Alpha chapter. God pointed them eastward to the University of Tennessee. The picturesque campus in Knoxville is bordered by the Great Smoky Mountains.

The change came at just the right time. U.S. missionary Chuck Lester pioneered the Chi Alpha group at Tennessee in 1997. Although two dozen other ministries existed on campus, none emphasized Holy Spirit-filled living. Lester in 2016 sought the Lord about handing off the Chi Alpha at Tennessee at the same time God talked to the Martins about branching out to a new location.

"Brooke and Tyler came to Tennessee with great faith, making a tremendous sacrifice to leave their families in Arkansas," Lester says.

The Martins went about implementing the DNA Lester had implanted.

"What we emphasize in Chi Alpha is small group discipleship: encouraging, equipping, and empowering students to share Jesus with other students," says the reflective Tyler, 30. "We invite students to follow us as we follow Jesus so they can make Him known here, there, and everywhere, regardless of the cost."

The Martins are accentuating the importance of global missions — going to the ends of the earth to make Jesus known. In all, 16 people connected with the University of Tennessee Chi Alpha have become full-time missionaries during the couple's six years at the school.

"We want to continue to have them leave us," says Brooke, 29. "We gather them for a season, but they serve God for a lifetime."

Tyler relates well to athletes at the school. He received a degree in physical education from the University of the Ozarks. Despite being only 5 feet, 5 inches tall, Tyler excelled on the school's basketball team as an excellent shooter. He also proved to be a spiritual leader, starting a Chi Alpha chapter on campus his junior year. By the time he graduated, 60 students — 10% of the enrollment — usually attended meetings. These days, he regularly is spotted playing ping pong or pool in the University of Tennessee student union.

Brooke, who earned a biblical studies degree at Evangel, says reading Robert E. Coleman's "The Master Plan of Evangelism" revolutionized her ministry thinking.

"Why had I been in church my whole life and never understood the vastness and severity of the Great Commission?" the articulate Brooke asks. "It's not just for when I get out of college, it's not just for when I get a job, it's not just for when I get older. We are God's soldiers who must urgently share the gospel. The Holy Spirit convinces students that they are the only way."

Ironically, in Tennessee and Arkansas — both considered part of the Bible Belt — Christianity is often culturally assumed rather than practically realized.

"Many students profess to be Christian when asked what religion they belong to, but in conversation it's evident they don't know what it is to follow Jesus," Tyler says.

"They're checking a box, but in reality, their god is self," Brooke says.

However, at Chi Alpha, many such students have their eyes spiritually opened.

"When they are exposed to the gospel, they see the deficiency in themselves and realize they need a Savior," Tyler says.

Tyler notes that students in the group have a heart for world missions. Earlier this year, 200 students donated $25,500 in a single offering to split between two staff couples being sent out as world missionaries.

One of the couples, Kyle and Porscha Coffman, also originally from Arkansas before joining the staff at the University of Tennessee four years ago, will spend a year in Mozambique training before pioneering somewhere on the African continent. The generosity of the collegiate donors overwhelmed them.

"I thought it would be one-tenth of that amount at most," says Kyle, 27. "The students are obedient to the Word of God."

"Brooke and Tyler modeled discipleship, showed they would stick with us, and gave us a launch pad into our next season of life," says Porscha, 27. "It is their desire and belief that if every person will disciple one student and multiply, all of the University of Tennessee will be reached with the gospel."

Lester, who now is Chi Alpha director for five universities in the Assemblies of God Tennessee Ministry Network, is an affirming supporter of the Martins.

"Brooke and Tyler are incredible disciplers and builders in the kingdom of God," says the enthusiastic Lester, 61. "God has brought quality students to them."

"Passion for World Evangelization. Brooke and Tyler Martin stress the magnitude of discipleship at the University of Tennessee Chi Alpha," by John W. Kennedy, originally appeared in *AG News*, Oct. 31, 2022.

STORY 10

Missouri University of Science & Technology in Rolla
Campus Ministers: Jason and Abigail Smith

As a student at Montana State University in Bozeman, Jason Smith struggled with depression and anxiety. His excessive drinking resulted in a forced semester off school, during which time he returned to his native Alaska.

While back home, Smith's newly born-again aunt Elizabeth Lauder told him about Jesus. Her joy impacted Smith profoundly.

"I had never seen anyone who loved Jesus before," recalls Smith, now 45. "I had never seen life in the Bible."

Invigorated, Smith returned to Montana State University with a newfound desire to serve the Lord. He joined the University Christian Fellowship, the local Chi Alpha Campus Ministries chapter then under longtime leader Dick Schroeder.

"I was discipled in that life-giving group," Smith remembers. "I walked through a lot of healing from depression and anxiety."

Although he sensed a call to ministry, Smith had managed to accumulate a sizable debt en route to an electrical engineering degree in 2002. So, he found good-paying work to reduce his financial obligations.

"God then gave me a tremendous job that I didn't deserve," Smith says. For the next 12 years, he worked at Los Alamos National Laboratory in New Mexico. He became part of the nuclear emergency response team; worked on quick response projects for the military, the FBI, and the CIA; and ended up working as lead engineer for an instrument on nuclear detention satellites. Along the way, Smith earned a master's degree in electrical engineering at the University of Missouri-Columbia.

With his career flourishing and while being groomed to be a national expert in the field of high voltage and space, Smith says his involvement with Chi Alpha at Mizzou rekindled the notion that the Lord had other plans.

"It's appropriate that a call to ministry should cost something," says Smith, a U.S. missionary.

Smith left his rewarding vocation to serve as a Campus Missionary-in-Training intern at Sam Houston State University in 2014. He served as Chi Alpha international outreach director at the school for an additional three years.

Then came an opportunity for Smith to combine his twin passions of electrical engineering and ministry.

In 2018, he restarted the Chi Alpha group at Missouri University of Science & Technology in Rolla, where future engineers and scientists are trained. Garrett and Emily Smith who also are U.S. missionaries, but not related to Jason, helped in the effort.

"I had thought about being a missionary overseas, but the Lord provided an avenue to go to an engineering school and see multiplication work," says Smith. "I want to push these students who have been dreaming about being an engineer their whole lives into seeking the Lord and how they can use their education on the mission field rather than just accepting the highest-paying job."

Smith opened a coffeeshop in Rolla in early 2022 to further his ministry goals of reaching people groups where it is difficult to preach the gospel.

"A coffeeshop can be opened about anywhere in the world," Smith says.

His long-term vision is to give engineers avenues to use their degree in the mission field.

"I want engineering students to have a place to do business as missions, and the coffeeshop is the first step toward starting business as missions entities," Smith says. "Is there a way these engineering graduates can go into the workforce with a bent toward missions to impact unreached people groups?"

With a team of students, Smith has launched an initial technical project to support an international partner, Water for All, a nonprofit company with a goal of providing clean, safe drinking water.

Smith and his wife of seven years, Abigail, along with Garrett and Emily Smith, have opened Coffeesmiths, a business in Rolla. Travellers House, a Springfield company owned by former national Chi Alpha administrative coordinator Cherie Venturella and her husband Greg, helped train the staff and provide expert advice about operating such a venture. The Venturellas are former AG world missionaries in Eastern Europe. Coffeesmiths, located in a renovated 130-year-old brick building, recently started serving breakfast and lunch.

Smith hopes the spot for coffee and tea is a blessing to the entire community, not just students.

"Coffeesmiths gives us unique opportunities to talk about Jesus with people we wouldn't have known otherwise," he says.

One of those impacted by Smith is Nigerian native Philip Olubodun, who graduated in the spring from Missouri S&T with a bachelor's degree in mechanical engineering. Olubodun met Smith at Rolla First Assembly of God just before Olubodun started classes at the school in 2018.

Olubodun joined a Chi Alpha small group and says Smith proved to be a good mentor and teacher. He appreciates that Smith always had time to answer questions, no matter how busy his schedule.

"Chi Alpha taught me the good news is meant to be shared," says Olubodun, now enrolled in a direct doctorate program at the school. "Developing relationships with Christians and non-Christians is a big mindset in Chi Alpha as way to spread the gospel around the world."

Abigail Smith, who met Jason at church in New Mexico, stays occupied helping with the ministry and raising the couple's four children.

"Engineering Twin Enthusiasms, Onetime Los Alamos Lab engineer Jason Smith leads Chi Alpha at a school for future engineers," by John W. Kennedy, originally appeared in *AG News*, Nov. 7, 2022.

STORY 11

University of California-Davis
Campus Ministers: Jennifer and Will Klier

Although the University of California-Davis is a highly nonreligious institution, U.S. missionaries and Chi Alpha Campus Ministries directors Will and Jennifer Klier believe a motto on the school's seal — "Let There Be Light" (Genesis 1:3) — is a prophetic call.

The UC-Davis campus has over 39,000 students from more than 100 nations, one of the most diverse student bodies in the U.S.

After the lockdown during the spring 2020 semester due to COVID-19, Chi Alpha remained the only student club or organization — out of more than 800 at UC-Davis — to be able to resume weekly in-person gatherings that summer. While on-campus get-togethers remained verboten, Chi Alpha could meet at its adjacent ministry property.

The ministry center purchased in 1999, as well as the discipleship house acquired in 2016, are at the busiest corner at the entrance to the school and feature large outdoor space for events. The nearly $1 million expansion of the discipleship house, paid for by donations from churches and individuals, provides a highly visible space next to a busy street with vehicles, bikes, and pedestrians. The Kliers, other Chi Alpha staff members, and student leaders invited masked students to participate in outdoor worship services.

The Kliers have led the ministry together for 17 years. Jennifer graduated from Western Washington University with a linguistics degree in 1997, completed a Campus Missionary-in-Training (CMIT) internship, served on the Western Washington University staff for a couple of years, and obtained her Assemblies of God ministerial credentials. She then transferred to the area of the country she considered the neediest spiritually: Davis, California.

At the time, Will — five years younger than Jennifer — attended school at UC-Davis. He joined the staff in 2002 after graduating, then served a CMIT at Montana State University in Bozeman for a couple of years while Jennifer led the Davis chapter alone. Will returned to UC-Davis in 2005, the year he married Jen.

"Davis students are bright, the cream of the crop," says the personable Will, 43. "But they have the same spiritual need we all have: the need for relationships."

"Students all want to make friends," echoes Jennifer, 48. "We've been able to build some trusting relationships."

Both raised on the West Coast, Will and Jennifer are familiar with a primary obstacle in ministering in a secular college setting: biblically illiterate students who lack a knowledge about God.

"We see the challenges as opportunities," Jennifer says. "We get to be the ones who share from scratch to atheists."

Some of the more receptive students are from outside the U.S. UC-Davis has an international student enrollment of more than 7,000. Some stay 10 weeks, others the entire four years. Every Friday night, the UC-Davis group hosts a "Conversation Hour" in which current Chi Alpha students seek to befriend international students through a theme or activity. Students share about American traditions and foreigners explain their customs.

Free food is a draw at many Chi Alpha gatherings. Marc Afshar transferred to UC-Davis as a junior. When a classmate invited him to a Chi Alpha progressive dinner event, Afshar, then an agnostic, gladly accepted. He says the affable approach taken by the Kliers toward him turned out to be life-changing.

"Will and Jennifer are available for students who are searching in their personal journey," says Afshar, 34. "No matter what stage a student is in, they make sure to introduce Jesus Christ and see that the student develops a personal walk with the Lord."

Afshar earned a biology degree at UC-Davis, part of his plan to become a pharmacist. But his involvement with Chi Alpha spurred a career switch to ministry.

"It completely shifted my paradigm of how to spend my life in something more meaningful," says Afshar, a U.S. missionary. After graduating in 2010, Afshar served on staff with the Kliers before setting out in 2016 to replant Chi Alpha at the University of the Pacific in Stockton, California. More than 50 UC-Davis alumni have served a year or more in missionary service in the U.S. or abroad.

The Kliers have three children. Will and Jennifer also have the opportunity to invest in students who already profess to be Christian.

Liane Henze grew up regularly going to church in the Bay Area. But during her first semester attending UC-Davis, she attended parties and drank alcohol most Thursday, Friday, and Saturday nights. A friend asked her to come to Davis Christian Fellowship (DCF), a Chi Alpha campus ministry large group service, and then she accepted Will's invitation to a fall retreat.

"It was the first time I really understood the gospel," recalls Henze, 29. Her life changed 180 degrees, and in subsequent years as a student she led DCF worship and core group Bible studies.

The Kliers became the most prominent figures in her life, Jennifer serving as her main mentor and Will being a father figure.

Henze graduated with an exercise biology degree with the intention of becoming a physical therapist. With her Christian mother and atheist father living in Taiwan, she agreed to give a year as a Chi Alpha intern. That was seven years ago. Liane is associate director for DCF and her husband of three years, Peter, also is on staff.

"Opening the Door to Relationships, Jennifer and Will Klier find a universal need on the UC-Davis campus," by John W. Kennedy, originally appeared in *AG News*, Nov. 22, 2022

STORY 12

University of Denver
Campus Ministers: Dan and Kayla Gibson

Dan Gibson spent most of his childhood in Mexico City as the son of Assemblies of God world missionaries Jerry and Gwen Gibson. He sensed a call to ministry himself at 15, and figured he would spend his life south of the U.S. border, the only context he knew.

Gibson graduated from Northwest University, the Assemblies of God school in Kirkland, Washington. He served a Chi Alpha Campus Missionary-in-Training internship at Stanford University in California. At the top-tier school, Gibson had the opportunity to invest in many future influencers.

Halfway through the internship in 2009, Gibson married Kayla Blair. The couple had met at Westminster Community Church in Shoreline, Washington, where Kayla served on the youth staff. In 2010, the Gibsons joined a team headed by Brad Novosad in pioneering Chi Alpha at the University of Colorado-Colorado Springs. In 2013, they became directors at the school, a role they maintained the next six years.

Still, the Gibsons felt they needed to learn more about team building, so in 2019 they moved to Fort Collins to help U.S. missionary Nate Banke, who had planted the Chi Alpha at Colorado State University a decade before. Dan served as diversity program director. Even though the Gibsons had three preschool-aged children at the time, Kayla decided to do a CMIT.

"Even though what seemed inconvenient at the time — with having three kids and learning what full time was like again — I now see the value of it," says Kayla, 35. "It was a sweet time being with younger interns, learning what true community was like. It helped us grow as parents and as a couple."

Although she grew up in the Fellowship, went on missions trips, participated in Fine Arts competitions, and felt called to ministry at 15, Kayla instead graduated from cosmetology school and worked at a salon for a living.

"Being on the Stanford campus and jumping into Dan's world was so overwhelming I felt like I could never minister to students there," Kayla remembers. "My involvement in campus ministry, while minimal initially, gradually grew until my full-time involvement at Colorado Springs. The details of life are so different than what I expected, in a challenging way."

At a prayer retreat, the Gibsons sought direction for their next step in ministry. They sensed the Lord impressing Proverbs 24:11 upon them — to rescue the perishing. Subsequently, they felt the Lord calling them to plant a Chi Alpha at the University of Denver, a school with 13,856 students. The chapter opened in September. Chad and Kendall Stogner — who served as interns with Kayla at Colorado State in 2019-20 — also are on the team. Like Stanford, the University of Denver is a prestigious private research school.

Whatever the collegiate setting, Gibson, a U.S. missionary, believes students are hungry for deep, caring friendships that Chi Alpha can provide.

"This generation is addicted to the phone, the clicks, the likes, having a curated life on Instagram and TikTok," says Gibson, 36. "There is little depth to their relationships."

But he expects to find students receptive to offers of a homey atmosphere.

"Community will be a key element of our ministry," Dan says. "We can invite students into our home." The Gibsons' three children are Bennett, Brielle, and Brynlee.

Banke, 40, notes that eight Chi Alpha chapters have been planted in Colorado in the past decade.

"We're all about ministries making ministries," says Banke, who serves as state Chi Alpha director in Colorado. He believes the Gibsons, assisted by their close friends the Stogners, who share similar convictions, will be effective pioneers at the University of Denver.

"Dan Gibson is high quality," Banke says. "His experience — both working at the elite Stanford as well as other pioneering efforts in the past — prepares him well."

Banke doesn't think Gibson will have difficulty adjusting to the potentially antagonistic environment.

"Dan is conscientious about ministering in a lot of different cultural dynamics," says Banke, noting his protégé's missionary kid origins. "His ability to be sensitive in sharing the gospel connects with people in a relational way. Students can tell he cares about them."

After serving for 24 years in Mexico as an AG world missionary, Jerry Gibson now is national director of Chi Alpha's Church Partnership Initiative to connect AG congregations to plant chapters on campuses.

"Pioneering in Denver, Seasoned couple Dan and Kayla Gibson launch a Chi Alpha in Colorado capital," by John W. Kennedy, originally appeared in *AG News*, Nov. 2, 2022.

STORY 13

Wright State University/Sinclair Community College, and University of Dayton, Ohio
Campus Ministers: Andy & Heather Erickson and Jay & Ashley Seidler

Four graduates of Wright State University in Ohio are taking a collaborative approach to ensure there is a Chi Alpha presence on campuses in the Dayton area.

U.S. missionaries Andy and Heather Erickson are focused on Wright State and Sinclair Community College, while Jay and Ashley Seidler are focused on the University of Dayton.

While the Chi Alpha groups at the schools allow for individual expression, by pooling resources and skills, the two married couples believe they can do ministry more effectively. In all, there are 11 Chi Alpha staff members at the trio of schools.

"We are able to reach more campuses working together than we would on our own," says Heather, 37.

"It's very taxing on an individual or married couple to try to do it all alone," says Ashley, 36. "Everything works better in a team. We all have different giftings."

The Ericksons and the Seidlers became friends in 2004 when they attended Chi Alpha events as students at Wright State. Andy graduated with an electrical engineering degree and found work at Wright-Patterson Air Force Base; Heather went into marketing for a restaurant franchise after earning a public relations degree.

Andy and Heather considered themselves mediocre Christians when they began their college studies, but four years attending Chi Alpha meetings changed not only their level of spirituality, but eventually their career path. When Wright State Chi Alpha leader U.S. missionary Steve Brannan left to become state director 11 years ago, the Ericksons knew God wanted them to step into the role, even though they walked away from lucrative careers. The couple, both U.S. missionaries, seem equally yoked and equally confident.

One of the distinctives of the Ericksons' ministry is encouraging students to read books by and about deceased Christian leaders such as Andrew Murray, A.W. Tozer, C.S. Lewis, Catherine Marshall, Corrie Ten Boom, and Elisabeth Elliott.

"We can learn a lot from the many men and women who have finished the full race with Jesus," says Andy, 37. "Today's society is inundated with new information, new methods, and new ways, but we need to learn from yesterday's Church. Old dead saints can help us understand Scripture."

"Everything we do is predicated on replicating Jesus' model of small group discipleship," says Heather, who is an executive presbyter with the Ohio Ministry Network. "We put everything into the transgenerational model of teaching our students to make disciples."

The Ericksons don't consider a student part of Chi Alpha unless he or she is committed to a small group: discipling peers, praying for the salvation of classmates, and seeking the baptism in the Holy Spirit for others in those gatherings.

"We want to empower young men and women to make disciples outside the college setting in any context: in their communities, with their neighbors, with their co-workers," Heather says. The Ericksons, who have a support team of four others, also believe it's important for students to give back. During their tenure, 27 students have participated in give-a-year opportunities either in the U.S. or in countries such as France, Peru, and Taiwan. Six alumni have served as short- or long-term missionary associates with AG World Missions.

Through the Campus Missionary-in-Training program, Chi Alpha alumni have served the Dayton area as worship leaders, youth pastors, and children's ministry workers. This fall, Jeffery and Olivia Palovchik committed to being marketplace missionaries in Alaska, working with U.S. missionaries Paul and Crystal Burkhart.

In a collaborative effort in June, Andy Erickson and Ashley Seidler led a 10-day Chi Alpha mission trip to Africa with seven students. Three students committed to full-time missions in the country as a result.

The trip, in an overwhelmingly Muslim-majority nation, primarily involved teaching English at a school while also encouraging existing missionaries and indigenous Christians. The experience inspired Erickson, who saw healings and other miracles.

"Seeing Muslims convert to Jesus permanently changed me," Erickson says. "They have forsaken family, jobs, and the future, and they experience persecution regularly. Yet they are committed to Jesus and are joyful. It's right out of the Book of Acts."

Ashley Seidler says she and Jay — a U.S. missionary and Ohio Ministry Network executive presbyter — hope every student involved in Chi Alpha at the University of Dayton will go on such a mission trip before graduating.

"We want to push our students to do things that are hard," Seidler says.

She is grateful that Heather Erickson influenced her as a first-year college student.

"I know Jesus because Heather invested in me," Seidler says. "Now we serve alongside each other and it's the best job in the world."

"Collaborating on Chi Alpha, Married couples join forces to reach schools around Dayton, Ohio," by John W. Kennedy, originally appeared in *AG News*, Dec. 9, 2022.

STORY 14

Boston colleges and universities
Campus Ministers: C. S. and Faith Robison

Boston, an important American city since the nation's colonial days, lately is renowned as a leading academic and scientific center. Forty educational institutions, including the prestigious Harvard University and Massachusetts Institute of Technology, call the greater urban area home.

The Assemblies of God Southern New England Ministry Network (SNE), led by Superintendent Nick W. Fatato, has embarked on a methodical and intentional strategy to launch a renewed effort to expand Chi Alpha Campus Ministries in the region. Fatato, 63, says research, recruiting, and resourcing are the guiding principles of the endeavor. He doesn't believe the proposal in Boston — the capital of Massachusetts and the largest city in New England — as too massive an undertaking.

"God is not intimidated by the vastness of Boston," says Fatato. "There are a quarter-million students and in four years there will be another quarter-million. The missional strategy to reach this population for impact in our region and around the world demands a large and visionary undertaking."

So far, 30 Chi Alpha team members have lined up to be a part of the task. Six already have moved to the Boston region.

Fatato, who earlier had a 20-year history in Chi Alpha, long believed the Church neglected two key places in the United States: metro areas and secular college campuses. Fatato worked as the first resident national field representative for Chi Alpha. Three decades ago, to model planting the first urban university national target, Fatato relocated to Boston with a team of six.

His vision has remained steady. Even before his election as SNE superintendent three years ago, Fatato led efforts to bring Chi Alpha into a strategic position in the region. He linked with three veteran Chi Alpha leaders who oversee large teams at the schools where they minister: U.S. missionary Anthony Saladino at Virginia Tech University; U.S. missionary Matt Carpenter at the University of Central Arkansas (UCA); and U.S. missionary Eli Gautreaux, Texas Chi Alpha leader who built the chapter at Sam Houston State University (SHSU).

The trio of directors are sending teams and helping steer the vision. They meet regularly with Fatato in person or via teleconferencing.

The planting team includes U.S. missionaries C.S. and Faith Robinson, who ethnically are Indians.

"The Robinsons bring years of experience and a deep passion for the work in Boston," Fatato says. "They are positioned well to help lead."

Formerly on staff at SHSU, the Robinsons moved to Boston's Mission Hill neighborhood, which has seven universities within a 1-mile radius. With supportive team members, the Robinsons hope to reach all the schools eventually. The largest is Northeastern University, a private research school, which has more than 2,100 students from India.

Because gaining access to public meeting space at private institutions can be challenging, the Robinsons, who are both 40 years old and ordained AG ministers, take a lifestyle evangelism approach.

"So many students live in the neighborhood apartments we technically don't need to get on campus to reach them," says C.S. born and raised in India. "The proximity and access is there, so we can form relationships."

"We see tons of opportunities to connect," says Faith, who grew up in a Pentecostal church in Houston. "Boston is a diverse city with students from all around the world."

C.S., also raised in Pentecostalism, earned a master's degree at New India Bible Seminary in Kerala and immigrated to the U.S. in 2008 — the same year he wed Faith in an arranged marriage.

The Robinsons responded to Fatato's appeal for Chi Alpha workers in 2019 after a visit to several campuses in Boston.

"It was a city full of students and young professionals," recalls C.S. "On a 10-minute walk, I heard seven languages spoken. I was overwhelmed."

Their immediate goal is to establish small group leaders who can form neighborhood relationships.

Faith received a bachelor's degree in education at SHSU and C.S. earned a second master's degree at the school in Huntsville, this one in sociology.

"Chi Alpha deepened my faith and I became open to the idea of a ministry career," says Faith, who gave a year as a missionary associate in the Netherlands after graduation.

Although a pastor's son, C.S. initially didn't expect to have a ministry career. He stuttered throughout childhood and youth, to such an extent that he had difficulty keeping friends. After he fully surrendered his life to the Lord at 21, he says God healed him of his speech impediment.

Subsequently, Acts 18:9-10 became a foundational encouragement verse for outreach in Boston. The passage tells of the Lord's vision assurance to the apostle Paul to keep proclaiming the gospel and not fear being harmed.

"Jesus has many people here in the city that He desires to raise up for Him," Faith says. "We're searching for God's people — who may not actually be God's people yet."

In addition to the Robinsons relocating to Boston, U.S. missionaries Michael and Rebekah Quinn have moved to Cambridge from UCA; U.S. missionary associate Steven Longoria and his wife, Alexandra, from the Stanford University Chi Alpha are finishing an internship at Yale University; and U.S. missionary Nick Huber has transferred from Virginia Tech.

"The Boston Massive Cure, Southern New England Ministry Network and Chi Alpha team up for strategic outreach to college students," by John W. Kennedy, originally appeared in *AG News,* Dec. 14, 2022.

STORY 15

New Mexico State University, Las Cruces
Campus Ministers: Daniel (Alex)* and Abby Rodriguez

Now in his fifth year as Chi Alpha Campus Ministries national training director, Alex Rodriguez is handling his responsibilities with aplomb.

His portfolio includes overseeing the annual Reach the University Institute, the annual Chi Alpha training conference and orientation for interns. He also is charged with directing the quadrennial Campus Missions Conference, where Chi Alpha directors, staff, and families gather for training and fellowship. The most recent get-together — in July 2022 in Phoenix — attracted a record 1,280 U.S. and world missionaries. The 37-year-old executive ministry team leader and U.S. missionary also is tasked with overseeing the Campus Missionary-in-Training internship program plus establishing core curricula for staff training.

Pastors habitually ask the muscular Rodriguez if he is paid as well as the retired 47-year-old baseball player with the same name who played 22 years in the American League and slugged 696 home runs. Like his baseball counterpart, the intense Rodriguez is a telegenic powerhouse.

The Chi Alpha A-Rod goes by his middle name. His first name is Daniel, but a plethora of Daniels in his kindergarten class prompted the switch. He grew up in the Houston area and his parents sent him to Christian schools because they wanted him to have a good education.

*Rodriguez currently serves as the national staff training director for Chi Alpha Campus Ministries, USA.

135

By the time he graduated high school, Rodriguez had memorized a multitude of Bible verses and knew an array of scriptural facts. But he viewed Jesus as a person in history, not a living Savior.

He wanted to take a break from religious instruction once he enrolled in college. In an effort to save money, he enrolled at the close-to-home and comparatively inexpensive Sam Houston State University (SHSU) in Huntsville, which had one of the largest Chi Alpha groups in the nation. But his girlfriend Abby (who has been his wife since 2009), invited him to a Chi Alpha small group meeting on campus. The language of the participants piqued his interest.

"People were speaking of Jesus in the present tense and how He talked to them," Rodriguez recalls. "This was a new experience for me."

Both Alex and Abby graduated in 2009 with kinesiology degrees. Alex originally intended to go into sports medicine to be an athletic trainer. But right after they married following graduation, the couple headed off to Central Asia as missionary associates on a Chi Alpha planting team. The ministry grew from seven to 70 followers during their time there. E. Scott Martin and his wife, Crystal, led the Central Asian team and discipled Alex and Abby for a year there.

After a stint on staff back at SHSU under the tutelage of U.S. missionaries Eli and Mary Gautreaux, Rodriguez planted the Chi Alpha chapter at New Mexico State University in Las Cruces.

Rodriguez gathered a capable team of 10 to help him launch at the campus, where half the students are Hispanic, as Rodriguez is.

"I did a lot of things wrong in the first year," the introverted Rodriguez reflects. "Everyone on staff had a job title, which created tensions." By year two, Rodriguez had dispensed with the job titles and told all his team to simply lead small groups. The chapter began to grow.

Chi Alpha has a place to meet on campus thanks to seed money provided by Radium Springs Family Worship Center, fundraising preaching events featuring Rodriguez, and the New Mexico Ministry Network making it a highlighted need. The combined efforts raised $100,000 as a down payment on a Chi Alpha student center at New Mexico State.

By the fifth year at the school, the Chi Alpha group had grown to 150 regular participants, making it the largest campus ministry at New Mexico State. Rodriguez felt a sense of accomplishment and satisfaction and saw no reason to leave.

But E. Scott Martin — who in 2014 became national Chi Alpha senior director — persuaded Rodriguez in 2018 to apply for the upcoming opening of national training director.

"In my time with him in Central Asia, I saw a young man with remarkable leadership potential who respected authority, paid honor to the Church, was hungry for the deeper things of God, and looked for the authentic gospel," remembers Martin, 60. "Alex had done an excellent job planting a team in New Mexico and we needed someone with his type of young leadership in a higher position."

Rodriguez sought the counsel of mentors, who split evenly whether he should remain in New Mexico or move to the national office in Springfield, Missouri.

Chi Alpha pioneer Harvey Herman urged Rodriguez to make the transition. Herman, a U.S. missionary who retired in January after 48 years of serving Chi Alpha in various roles, had been looking for a replacement for his roles as training and internship director.

Herman says Rodriguez gained much credibility because of interning at SHSU, committing to give a year at a university in a foreign country, and launching a now-thriving ministry in a tough environment at New Mexico State.

"Alex is successful in university ministry because people listen to him," Herman says. "He is an articulate and careful speaker who doesn't waste words."

Herman notes that Rodriguez conducted a retreat at Yale University, where Herman's daughter Sarah Malcolm is co-director with her husband, Rob.

"Alex is able to speak eloquently and effectively at an academically elite school as well as a small state school," Herman says. "He knows his individual audience."

Rodriguez accepted the national position after listening to a sermon by AG world missionary Dick Brogden about seeking more of Jesus.

"Leaving the familiar and comfortable has led me to more of Jesus," Rodriguez says. "This job is the hardest thing I've ever done."

To make the transition easier, Rodriguez convinced four team members to transfer with him from the Land of Enchantment: U.S. missionary associate Sarah Aitken; appointed U.S. missionary Derek Lynn and his wife, Natalia; and Christina Winters. All have filled national support staff roles in Missouri.

Martin says Rodriguez has exceeded his expectations. He notes that the Chi Alpha group at New Mexico state is even larger than when Rodriguez served as director because Rodriguez discipled staff well.

As he looks to the future in his national role, Rodriguez is focused on ensuring that the divergent chapters are on the same page.

"Chi Alphas don't all look the same or behave the same," Rodriguez says. "My job is to cultivate a common culture across uncommon campuses."

His four priorities of training for healthy Chi Alpha campuses are:

- Holy Spirit empowerment, including spiritual gifts and speaking in tongues
- Cross-cultural missions
- Healthy leaders
- Disciple-making groups.

"These will manifest themselves in different ways at different campuses," Rodriguez says. "They are identical principles, but not necessarily identical practices."

As a Hispanic, Rodriguez also provides leadership diversity at the national level that the ministry is endeavoring to replicate on campuses around the country.

While the national training director portfolio is established, Martin wanted to give Rodriguez some leeway in other aspects of the job. Subsequently, Rodriguez is developing continuing education and professional development training for veteran campus directors.

As if he isn't busy enough, Rodriguez just finished writing the second book of a trilogy, *Real Community: Learning to Love One Another*. His first book is *Real Devotion*, while the third planned text is *Real Responsibility*. Rodriguez says the publications contain biblical truths he learned at SHSU.

Rodriguez says the prayers of many Chi Alpha friends are responsible for Abby giving birth to "miracle daughter" Wesley Kate two years ago after seven years of infertility. Abby remains involved in Chi Alpha, helping to process intern applications as well as assisting the personnel department with records coordination.

Martin considers Rodriguez a beloved younger brother.

"I knew he would excel because of his character, capabilities, and fruitfulness," Martin says. "He is an excellent analytic thinker and a brilliant writer."

"Discipleship Legacy, Chi Alpha training director Daniel (Alex) Rodriguez sees the need for developing staff, from interns to veterans," by John W. Kennedy, originally appeared in *AG News*, Dec.19, 2022.

Another book by Dennis Gaylor published in 2021

Growing a Student Movement, The Development of Chi Alpha Campus Ministries, 1940–2020

Dennis Gaylor writes a 656-page chronological history of Chi Alpha from its beginnings to the present day. Chi Alpha is the campus ministry of the Assemblies of God on secular campuses. Gaylor, who served as national Chi Alpha director for 34 years, offers an in-depth portrait of the ministry from its humble origins to the explosive growth of recent years, both nationwide and internationally.

Dennis, uniquely qualified to write a history of Chi Alpha, lived and formed much of it. The story is brought to life through an introduction, eight chapters by decades, three chapters on world missions, international student ministry, and a parallel historical account of university ministry outside the U.S., and three other

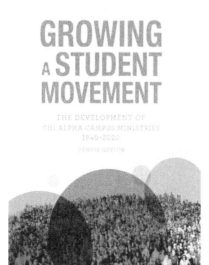

chapters on change, new leadership, and spiritual awakening, and ends with an epilogue about the year 2020. In *Growing a Student Movement* there are 650 photographs and 65 charts. The reader can know the history, experience the present, and have a view of the future of Chi Alpha.

Available @ Amazon.com for $19.95

Endorsements:

An Insider's View Dennis Gaylor provides an insider's view of the history of Chi Alpha — an important record of service and sacrifice in the mission of reaching generations of university students for Christ. Perhaps no one has done more than Dennis to build Chi Alpha into a premier national campus ministry, but the significant contributions of all his cohorts find their place here.
Joseph Castleberry — Ed. D. President, Northwest University

The Incredible Journey of Chi Alpha
Dennis Gaylor thoroughly documents the incredible journey of Chi Alpha, as it advanced far beyond the vision of its founders to become a fountainhead of ambassadors for Christ in missionary service throughout the world — more than its founders could have asked or imagined. It is inspiring and instructive reading!
Randy Hurst — advancement director for Assemblies of God World Missions

The Greatest Untold Story
One of the greatest untold stories in the Assemblies of God has now been told. *Growing a Student Movement* is a detailed account of the growth and impact of Chi Alpha Campus Ministries. Nobody could tell this story better than Dennis Gaylor. His experience, perspective, and long-term commitment to the movement equips him to chronicle this profound story. Every page unpacks this ministry that is impacting the campus, marketplace and the world.
Nick Fatato — network superintendent Southern New England Ministry Network of the Assemblies of God

What God is Doing on the Campus
One cannot read *Growing a Student Movement* without witnessing the love, enthusiasm, and dedication of college students and campus pastors in their commitment to be Christ's Ambassadors.

Unprecedented in scope and rich in detail, this book will inspire every Assemblies of God pastor, campus minister and XA member to expand their vision of what God can do in today's world.

Dr. James F. Cobble, Jr. — Board of Advisers Gordon-Conwell Theological Seminary